Supply Chain Management

v/d|f

vdf Hochschulverlag AG
an der ETH Zürich

Ralf Hieber

Supply Chain Management

A Collaborative Performance Measurement Approach

Edited by
Prof. Dr. Paul Schönsleben

Center for Enterprise Sciences
Swiss Federal Institute
of Technology (ETH) Zurich
Zürichbergstrasse 18
CH-8028 Zürich

**Research Reports
for Industrial Practice
Domain Prof. Dr. Paul Schönsleben
www.lim.ethz.ch**

Volume 12

Die Deutsche Bibliothek – CIP-Einheitsaufnahme

Hieber, Ralf:
Supply chain management : a collaborative
performance measurement approach /Ralf Hieber.
Hrsg. von Paul Schönsleben.
– Zürich : vdf, Hochschulverlag an der ETH, 2002
(vdf Wirtschaft)
Zugl.: Zürich, Eidgenössische Techn. Hochsch.,
Diss., 2001
ISBN 3-7281-2832-5

ISBN 3 7281 2832 5

Introduction by the series editor

Many complex value-added chains have become popular in the last two decades, not least due to the consistent reduction of production levels in companies. This has lead to a situation where many companies are co-operating in order to develop and manufacture a saleable product. The resulting ups and downs have also created the need for the successful and economical management of such supply chains. Meanwhile, logistics networks and their management have been the focus of many research efforts. In the recent past, some contributions on how to measure the performance of logistics networks have also appeared. And, while systematic characteristics and logistics performance indicators for the measurement of internal operations efficiency have been available for decades, for logistics networks, it is mostly of case of starting from scratch.

Dr. Hieber's work has arrived at the right moment. It isn't enough to simply reassemble all of a company's internal indicators on the level of a logistics network. The author develops a model to measure the performance of logistics networks and differentiates between the so-called generic performance indicators and the aggregate indicators that can be adapted from the company's internal performance measurements. All these indicators and the supporting definitions and processes are ultimately used to expand the SCOR model that was formulated and presented in 1996 by the Supply Chain Council (SCC).

This work describes the distinguishing features of the performance between the companies and as such makes an important contribution to the effectiveness and efficiency of the network. An approach that is well-known in corporate logistics, that is, building up the logistics-related characteristics in the form of morphological scheme is also applied to mapping the characteristics for the external logistics network.

This book makes a breakthrough contribution to transcorporate logistics, namely, a broad overview of the subject as well as useful tools for measuring the performance of logistics networks – as an expansion of the performance measurement of the various companies internal logistics. The integration of the results into an accepted environment (SCOR) ensures that its spread is optimal.

The excellent results are not only the culmination of years of cooperation with industry on various projects, which also presents a decisive argument for the practical application of the results, but also the outcome of the effective use of an international research network that Dr. Hieber carefully created and supported. This is one of the reasons why – and it is particularly a great pleasure for me – this work is being published in English.

Zurich, January 2002   Prof. Dr. Paul Schönsleben

Preface

For over a decade, there has been a growing interest in the concept of supply chain management to improve performance across the entire logistics network. Most companies have realized that the efficiency of their own businesses is heavily dependent on their external relationships because of the more and more complex, linked value-adding processes between business network partners. Thus, the concept of supply chain management strives for the seamless integration of the activities associated with the flow and transformation of goods in transcorporate logistics through improved supply chain relationships between the network entities. However, although the benefits of SCM are well-known in industry, companies, especially SME, have as yet only put this concept into practice in a limited way. Therefore, the newly developed integral model of collaborative performance measurement in this book will make a contribution to support improvements in transcorporate logistics as well as to give specific guidelines for the implementation of SCM.

In the first part of the book, respective logistics characteristic features of logistics networks in the relevant dimensions of collaboration, coordination and configuration are identified, which then allow the specification of the current state of transcorporate logistics. Based upon these characteristic features, a common network understanding and logistics knowledge between the logistics partners can be achieved.

In the second part of the book, current performance measurement approaches were evaluated with respect to their appropriateness for supporting a network performance measurement approach, i.e., preventing single local optimization instead of striving for a global network optimum. Most advanced in this area is the SCOR model, which therefore serves as a basis for the new two-phase integral model proposed for performance measurement, consisting of generic high-level and aggregated corporate performance indicators, as well as including specific implementation guidelines.

In the first phase of the model, the identified high-level generic performance indicators will help set the baseline for common supply chain improvements by addressing the enable-oriented network performance target areas of collaboration, coordination and transformability excellence. In a second phase, by building up trust and openness in the relationships, the performance measurement then can be enlarged by aggregating and transforming existing SCOR metrics on a network level towards addressing the more result-oriented network performance target areas of costs, assets, reliability, responsiveness and flexibility of SCOR.

In summary, by combining the two sets of performance indicators as well as the proposed guidelines, a powerful tool is provided for an integral performance measurement approach for logistics networks.

Acknowledgements

This book is a slighty changed version of my Ph.D. thesis which arose during my assistantship as a researcher in the group Logistics and Information Management under Prof.Dr. Paul Schönsleben at the Center for Enterprise Sciences (BWI) of the Swiss Federal Institute of Technology (ETH) in Zürich. It is based on the extended results of the ProNet research project funded by the Commission of Technology and Innovation (CTI). Many people have contributed to this work in various ways, members of the BWI, research and industry partners as well as students who helped me throughout the realization of this work and thus made it possible.

I would like to thank my advisor and thesis examiner, Prof.Dr. Paul Schönsleben, for his scientific support and high degree of academic freedom as well as the generous amount of trust and pleasant cooperation, which made it possible for me to conduct my research in an independent way.

I would also like to thank Prof.Dr. Rémy Glardon, Director of the Laboratoire de Gestion et Procédés de Production (LGPP) of Ecole Polytechnique Federale de Lausanne (EPFL), for taking over the part of co-examining the thesis and the discussion on the thesis subject.

Furthermore, this work was possible only through the intensive collaboration with the project partners of Huber+Suhner Ltd., DiverseyLever Ltd., IBM, FOLAG, PEKA and USCO SA. A special thanks therefore to Daniel Böhm, Dr. Oliver Boxler, and Peter Rehm of Huber+Suhner, and Markus Schneider and Kurt Portmann of DiverseyLever, and Francis Kuhlen of IBM for mentoring, promoting and extensively supporting this project.

I also extend my sincere thanks to Prof.Dr. Claudio Boër of CTI (Commission for Technology and Innovation) and the Swiss Federal Office for Professional Education and Technology for their help in supporting this dissertation in the scope of the project ProNet, as well as all ProNet Team members, especially Robert Alard, Dieter Fischer, Brigitte Gonzalez, Michel Pouly and Anna Windischer.

Finally, my thanks go to my parents whose support and encouragement during all the years of studies made this work possible in the first place.

Zurich, January 2002   Ralf Hieber

Table of contents

List of acronyms and abbreviations

ALP	Advanced Logistic Partnership
APICS	American Production and Inventory Control Society
APS	Advanced Planning and Scheduling
BSC	Balanced Scorecard
CPFR	Collaborative Planning, Forecasting and Replenishment
CR	Continuous Replenishment
ECR	Efficient Consumer Response
EDI	Electronic Data Interchange
EFQM	European Foundation for Quality Management
ENAPS	European Network for Advanced Performance Studies
ERP	Enterprise Resource Planning
ICT	Information and Communication Technology
IT	Information Technology
MRP	Material Requirement Planning
PPC	Production Planning and Control
MRPII	Manufacturing Resource Planning
QR	Quick Response
SCC	Supply Chain Council
SCM	Supply Chain Management
SCOR	Supply Chain Operations Reference Model
SME	Small and Medium-sized Enterprises
TQM	Total Quality Management
VDI	Verein Deutscher Ingenieure
VMI	Vendor Managed Inventory
XML	Extensible Markup Language

List of figures

List of tables

1

1 Introduction to the research field

1.1 Motivation

Since the early 1980s, there has been an increasing interest in the concept of supply chain management (SCM) to improve performance across the entire industrial logistics network and hence, over these two decades, supply chain management has become a standard part of the business literature and research agendas. Companies that have already streamlined their internal business processes are now working on optimizing their external relationships to their business partners by using new information and communication technology (ICT) and initiating innovative logistics concepts. Globally active companies, as well as small and medium-sized enterprises (SME), which are more and more part of these complex logistics networks, have realized that the efficiency of their own businesses is heavily dependent on external collaboration and coordination with their suppliers as well as their customers. From this realization emerged the concept *supply chain management*, which is concerned with the strategic approach of dealing with *logistics planning and operation on an integrated basis*[1]. Nowadays, companies must also be involved in the logistics management of the network of all upstream companies, as well as the network of downstream companies responsible for delivery and customer service to the end consumer.[2] This interest increased significantly when companies saw both the benefits of business partnerships and the threats of 'isolation' as well as the emergence of

---

[1] Lau/Lee, 2000, p. 598.

[2] Handfield, 1999, p. 2.

new and promising information and communication technologies (e.g., Internet), which now enable new ways of managing business partnerships. As a consequence, supply chain management, an integral approach of linking suppliers, producers and customers together for collaborative management of the logistics network, is a crucial element for increasing competitiveness, better customer care and quicker response in today's marketplace.

1.2   The need for transcorporate performance measurement in logistics networks

The supply chain management concept fundamentally changes the nature of organizations. Logistics management is no longer based on direct ownership and control, but rather on collaboration and coordination across company boundaries as well as interfaces between different departments and different functions, which also finally affects the performance measurement approaches in place. As a matter of fact, both practitioners and research scientists noted a number of issues regarding measurement activities[3] in supply chain management early on. The issues reported suggest that measurement activities are fragmented both within and across organizations as well as being too focused on short-term performance perspectives, mainly cost and time. Furthermore, improper use of performance measurement systems and the lack of supply chain performance indicators can be a barrier to the implementation of transcorporate logistics concepts.[4]

In more detail, there are several main problem areas related to performance measurement identified in research[5]. First, there are few performance indicators, which incorporate integrated transcorporate processes in logistics networks. Most indicators are related to single activities and functions in the supply chain. Only some can be combined into a more integrated view by simply adding the corresponding metrics of subsequent network entities, which then results in total response time, cash-to-cash cycle time or total inventory level[6], in order to avoid optimization at one point in the network without considering potential conse-quences at other points in the network. Second, existing traditional logistics performance measurement approaches do not address the crucial combination of integrated and non-integrated indicators. By giving a supply chain member measurement information on their own performance (non-integrated) as well as performance of the whole network (integrated), the partners can assess the overall competitiveness of the network as a whole, while still enabling them to focus on improvement efforts for their own performance[7]. This will lead to more

---

[3]   MELNYK/CALANTONE, 1999.

[4]   LEE/BILLINGTON, 1992, p. 65.

[5]   BECHTEL/JAYARAM, 1997, p. 24.

[6]   SCOR level 1 metrics in Appendix C.

[7]   HOEK V., 1998, p. 189.

incentives to 'team-up' and to strive for a global network optimum. Hence, the internal performance measurement is still mandatory and, in general, tends to have a corporate perspective, while the network performance measurement should support a more generic transcorporate logistics perspective.

Therefore, traditional performance measurement approaches may have to be enhanced and attention directed more towards a logistics network approach. Thus, innovative ways of collaborative performance measurement must be developed and new performance dimensions must be taken into consideration that go beyond the traditional dimensions like cost, time and quality.

1.3   Research goal and objectives

The research goal of this work is to make a contribution to the improvement of transcorporate logistics in industrial networks. Based on existing approaches and techniques of performance measurement, an integral model should be developed to enable and support the transcorporate performance measurement.

The most crucial issue of isolated optimization of single entities of a network should thereby be overcome and the overall competitiveness of the network as a whole should be addressed. Therefore, integrated logistics performance indicators assigned to relevant dimensions of a network across functional areas and organizational boundaries must be provided.

As a matter of fact, this measurement approach must be developed collaboratively and must enhance the current approaches in practice, which use costs as a primary (if not sole) performance indicator. Hence, return-on-investment (ROI) and head counts can no longer be considered as the sole key performance indicator in a logistics network. Those measures can be appropriate and suitable in an organization with direct ownership, in which the management has direct access to all necessary data, however, for the evaluation of the performance of a logistics network formed by independent business organizations, a new collaborative approach must be developed, which provides the members in the network with a framework that allows the flexibility and ability to jointly develop the performance indicators in a supply chain context. In addition, by using this methodology, the members of the logistics network should get more awareness of their transcorporate interdependencies and business relationships.

The scientific objective of the work is to evaluate the current approaches to performance measurement regarding the new transcorporate logistics requirements and to find new and innovative ways of collaborative performance measurement.

The following steps support this objective:

- Characteristic features for describing the relevant dimensions of a logistics network must be determined to demonstrate the crucial specialties as well as to characterize the current integral logistics state of a network. This must be on a high level to guarantee the adaptability to logistics networks, regardless of industry branch, type and size.

- Based on the complexity and uniqueness of logistics networks, a framework for a scaleable, adaptive and systematic approach for performance measurement should be provided, which extends the existing approaches to a more integral approach and encompasses all relevant dimensions of a logistics network. The focus hereby will be mainly on strategic high level performance indicators.

- Guidelines should be proposed that facilitate the implementation of the recommended framework.

- The new performance measurement approach should lead the way for collaborative network competitiveness and should direct management attention to areas for network improvements.

1.4   Structure of the book

The structure of the book can be classified in two main parts. The first part addresses the state-of-the-art of transcorporate logistics, whereas the second part is mainly dedicated to innovative ways of performance measurement, which finally leads to an enhancement of the SCOR methodology.

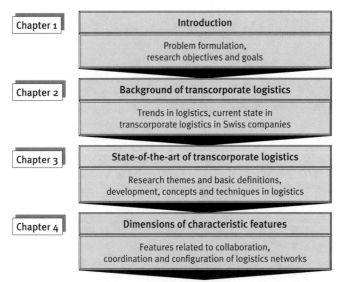

Figure 1-1:   Part A addresses the state-of-the-art in transcorporate logistics

In chapter 1, the basic research directions will be defined and the primary problem formulation stated, which gives the basis for the research objectives and scope of the work. In chapter 2, the background and traditional issues in transcorporate logistics will be highlighted. The innovation drivers especially, and the substantial shifts in industrial environment will be described, which have finally led to this far-reaching development. To reveal the practical relevance of this research field, the result of a survey in the context of supply chain management will be presented. In chapter 3, basic definitions and the underlying understanding of logistics in this dissertation will be discussed to clarify the scope of an integral performance measurement. At the end of part A, relevant respective characteristic features of logistics networks will be presented in chapter 4.

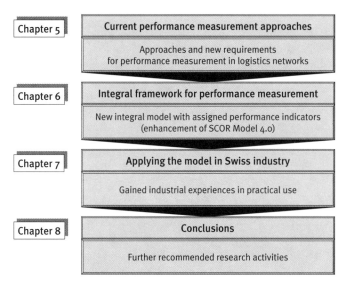

Figure 1-2:   Part B addresses new approaches to performance measurement

Chapter 5 gives a brief overview of current performancemeasurement approaches and evaluates their appropriateness for industrial logistics networks. In addition, the chapter will summarize the basic principles on collaborative performance measurement. In chapter 6, a new model to meet the identified requirements on a new performance measurement approach in respect to the dimensions of collaboration, coordination and transformability excellence, including assigned generic performance indicators, will be proposed using SCOR as a basis. To validate the proposed integral model, in chapter 7 the approach will be applied in two case studies in Swiss industry to demonstrate its applicability as well as the experiences gained. Finally, further recommendations for research directions will be highlighted in chapter 8.

2 Background of transcorporate logistics

In this chapter the background and the traditional issues in transcorporate logistics will be highlighted. The initiators and the drivers of this fairly new concept, at the beginning especially, will be discussed, as well as the major substantial shifts in the industrial environment which led to this new development. Finally, to reveal the practical relevance of this research field, the results of a survey in the context of supply chain management will be presented, which demonstrate the current state-of-the-art in transcorporate logistics in the Swiss industry.

2.1 Trends in transcorporate logistics

The acceleration in the globalization of the marketplace, increasing expectations concerning customer service quality, the building of global alliances and partnerships[8], the limited availability of resources in the future, and the impact of information and communication technologies (ICT) had forced companies to look beyond their own organizational boundaries. All these changes in the industrial environment and more demanding customers had a significant impact on the integral logistics management, which led to new challenging requirements on the collaboration, coordination, and transformability of logistics networks (see chapter 6).

In figure 2-1, these above-mentioned drivers and changes are summarized and will be then discussed in more detail.

---

[8] WOMACK/JONES/ROOS, 1990, p. 48.

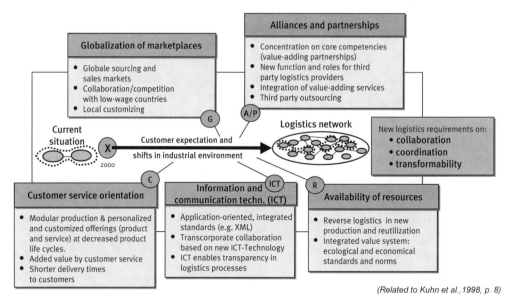

(Related to Kuhn et al.,1998, p. 8)

Figure 2-1:   Trends and changes in the industrial environment

2.1.1   Globalization of the marketplace

One of the strategic issues that provides a challenge for logistics management is the trend towards globalization. In global business, material and components are sourced worldwide, manufactured in several production sites around the world, and sold in many different countries, perhaps with local customization. Therefore, companies form global logistics networks, in which SME are also more and more integrated to serve customers all over the world. By coordinating spread production, distribution and service units, global companies are able to offer best-of-class customer service in a reasonable response time. As a consequence, companies that can most effectively gather and act upon vital information along the whole supply chain up to the end customer are gaining great competitive advantages. Hence, for these globally active enterprises, the management of the logistics processes has become an issue of central concern.

2.1.2   Information and communication technology (ICT)

IT innovations have developed at a breathtaking pace over last decade. First of all, the rapid spread of Internet technology, the progress in network technology itself, which allows access to the Web from almost anywhere, and, as a consequence, the huge number of resulting Internet applications, such as e-commerce (electronic) or m-commerce (mobile) tools, are the enabling technologies for global business and transactions among companies. Moreover, the steady increase of computing power and, at the same time, the declining price of hardware have recently made new software solutions possible, like advanced planning and scheduling (APS) and supply chain network planning applications (see section 3.5.1). Hence, the technology for optimizing complex networks and supply chains is available at a reasonable price for a large number of companies. Presently, software vendors, such as SAP, i2 technologies, Manugistics, and JDEdwards are seizing the opportunity, discovering huge market potentials for this kind of software application and expecting a tremendous growth rate[9].

2.1.3   Customer service orientation

The focus of today's business marketplace is on creating value through personalized and customized offerings, not just of products, but also of services, targeted to individual customers rather than 'one size fits all' products. Furthermore, because of the wealth of information available (e.g., Internet), customers continue to become more demanding and, as a consequence, the balance of power is more and more shifting toward the customers. Where a customer perceives little technical difference between competing offerings, the need is for creation of differential advantages through added value, and a prime source can be customer service. Those companies that have already achieved recognition for service excellence (e.g., Dell Computers) are typically those companies where logistics management is a high priority. The attainment of service excellence in this broad sense can only be achieved through a closely integrated logistics strategy.[10]

2.1.4   Limited availability of resources

Reverse logistics will play a major role in the near future to support new products and production concepts also forced by legal requirements, by guaranteeing the reutilization of the assembled components and resources. The development of integrated value systems will emerge because of changing ecological and economical standards and norms in society. To manage the challenge of economic and ecological life cycles especially, intelligent networks must be set up and organized. Furthermore, all life cycle stages such as product development and design, manufacturing, marketing, using, servicing, recycling and disposal must be harmonized under consideration of CO_2 emission reduction, resource and sustainable product management[11]. Thus, this development will additionally force the building of 'reverse' logistics networks.

---

[9]   AMR 2000.

[10]   CHRISTOPHER, 1998, p. 24.

[11]   HIEBER, M., 2000.

2.1.5   Alliances and partnerships

As one of the major results of the tendency to concentrate on the core competencies in industry, companies are striving increasingly for value-adding partnerships. Thereby, more and more companies are discovering the advantages that can be gained by seeking mutually beneficial and long-term relationships with their suppliers. From the suppliers' point of view, such partnerships can prove a formidable barrier to entry for competitors. The more processes are linked between the supplier and customer, the more mutual dependencies exist and hence the more difficult it is for competitors to break in.[12] Especially for small and medium-sized companies, this will be a big opportunity to resist big competitors. By simply sharing their skills as well as combining and enlarging their production capabilities, new business opportunities can be developed. In the following, this collaboration between independent and equal business partners will be referred to as supply chain networks (compare section 4.2.3).

2.2   Main issues in logistics networks

In the following paragraph, the main issues in industrial logistics networks will be discussed. First, a well-known issue in transcorporate logistics, the Bullwhip Effect, will be covered. This has been one of the key starting points for numerous supply chain management research activities, ones which finally ended up with new organizational concepts (see section 3.4) and SCM software support (see section 3.5). Nowadays, the focus in research is directed more towards overall performance measurement in order to overcome a second major issue, the single optimization of network entities, mainly resulting from the current performance measurement systems in place (see chapter 5).

2.2.1   Dynamics and uncertainty in logistics networks

A frequent and painful phenomenon in logistics networks is upstream order magnification, known as the Bullwhip Effect or Forrester Effect. While customer demand for specific products does not vary much, inventory levels and order quantities fluctuate considerably across the supply chain. The more partners are involved over several subsequent value-adding levels in jointly satisfying the demand of the final customer, the more uncertainty is transmitted onto the next stage in the logistics network as a consequence of delay, noise and bias. FORRESTER first simulated the demand amplification characteristic exhibited by real-world supply chains over forty years ago. More recently, this phenomenon has become known as the 'Bullwhip Effect'. MASON-JONES and TOWILL describe this phenomenon:

---

[12]   CHRISTOPHER, 1998, p. 33.

"If demand for products is transmitted along a series of inventories using stock control ordering, then the demand variation will increase with each transfer."[13]

Thus, much uncertainty is system induced and magnified by the Bullwhip Effect, as opposed to being introduced by the final customer or the marketplace.[14] Figure 2-2 demonstrates clearly the effect along a supply chain by comparing the order patterns and the inventory levels as a function over time along the value chain.

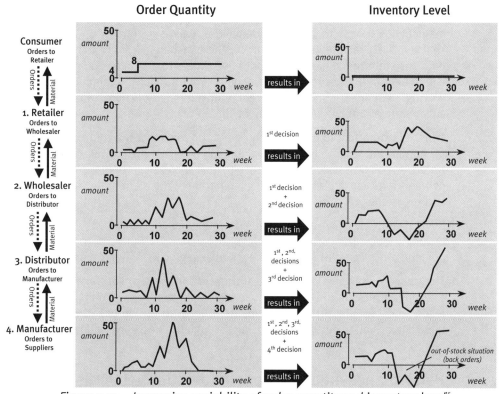

Figure 2-2:   *Increasing variability of order quantity and inventory level*[15]

Most of these findings and experiences had their origin in the distribution logistics of the consumer packaged goods (CPG) industry, where mainly simple one-to-one delivery relationships over several supply chain tiers exist.[16] Nowadays, more and more production and procurement aspects have been integrated in these studies, where similar effects can be observed.

---

[13]   MASON-JONES/TOWILL, 2000, p. 41.

[14]   MASON-JONES/TOWILL, 2000, p. 40.

[15]   These are results of the logistics simulation game "Beer-Game", originated from MIT, and also observed as well as analyzed in several logistics networks in practice in the project ProNet funded by the Swiss Commission for technology and innovation (CTI), contract nos. 4209 and 4674.1.

[16]   Most famous example is the demand for Pampers disposal diapers, which was analyzed and published in several journals by Procter & Gamble.

An excellent means of demonstrating the Bullwhip Effect as an increase in variability up the supply chain, is the 'Beer-Game'[17], which is representative of a four tier supply chain. The objective is to minimize cumulative costs over the length of the game due to excess inventory and stock outs (back orders). Each player receives an individual order from the previous player, except the retailer, who receives a fixed order amount from the 'market' and delivers accordingly, from which he makes a decision on what to order from his subsequent player. As a matter of fact, each player tries to anticipate demand and balance inventory. The above figure shows some sample results, and as expected, highlights the magnified response to consumer demand at each step further up in the supply chain. In fact, for the scenario shown, the consumer demand pattern changes only once during the game, and that is stepwise from a order quantity of four to eight. Although the consumer demand is very stable and 'simple', the wildly varying responses show the real difficulty in uncoordinated and less collaborative supply chain decision making.

Thus, it is important to identify techniques and tools that will control the increase in variability in supply chains. As LEE and many further researchers have demonstrated, the main factors contributing to this increase in demand variation are demand forecast updating, order batching, price fluctuation and rationing, and shortage gaming.[18]

Several strategies have already been developed to cope with these issues. These include reducing uncertainty, reducing the variability inherent in the customer demand process, reducing lead times, and engaging in strategic partnerships.[19]

The ultimate objective of all these approaches is the seamless integration of all relevant partners in the network, wherein all players 'think and act as one'. This leads finally to one of the key elements of most of the proposed concepts – to reduce information delay for improving the logistics decision-making process.

2.2.2   Performance measurement in logistics networks

An additional serious issue in industrial logistics networks is the isolated optimization of single nodes of the entire network, which mostly results from the performance indicators already in place. Although the logistics network overall performance results form the joint performance of each network partner, usually each site is managed by fairly autonomous management teams, each with its own performance indicators. The consequence will be isolated optimization, which can be even counterproductive to the overall performance of the network. Studies revealed that overall performance indicators are seldom in place and if, then the overall performance was measured in oversimplified and sometimes

---

[17]   The game and its environment is described in great detail by STERMAN, 1989, pp. 321–339.

[18]   LEE ET AL., 1997, p. 95.

[19]   SIMCHI-LEVI ET AL., 2000, p. 91.

counterproductive (cost-reduction based) terms.[20] The lack of an appropriate performance measurement has been cited as a major obstacle to effective collaboration in logistics networks.[21] In transcorporate logistics, timely and accurate assessment of overall system performance as well as individual system component performance is of a paramount importance. An effective performance measurement system (1) provides a basis for understanding the system, (2) influences behavior throughout the system, and (3) provides information regarding the results of system efforts to network members and outside stakeholders.[22] Therefore, in chapter 5, current practices of performance measurement will be discussed and finally, in chapter 6, new innovations towards a collaborative and network-oriented approach are presented.

2.2.3   Main issues in Swiss logistics networks

To reveal the practical relevance and demonstrate the perceived main issues in the area of transcorporate logistics, mainly from general managers of SME, figure 2-3 shows the result of a survey in Swiss industry.[23] On top, insufficient trust in the network is mentioned. Most of the managers still fear sharing information with their partners with the assumption that the business partners can misuse this information (e.g., with its competitors) and therefore, as the results show, many supply chain relationships witness limited information exchange (see figures 2-10 and 2-11). With the same high rank, poor planning opportunities is mentioned related to the lack of information and uncertainty in the network. Further practical insights are the lack of IT compatibility, the high amount of management resources which SCM concepts require, the fear of high dependency, the lack of communication and cultural differences, to mention the most often stated answers. In general, these findings give interesting insights into the practical issues in transcorporate logistics.

---

[20]   HANDFIELD, 1999, p. 62.

[21]   LALONDE/POHLEN, 1996, p. 4. and LEE/BILLINGTON, 1992, p. 65.

[22]   FACETT/CLINTON, 1996, pp. 40–46.

[23]   HIEDER ET AL., 2000.

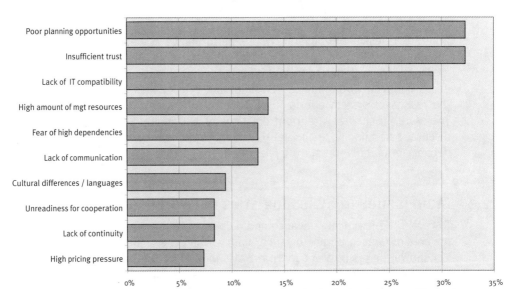

Figure 2-3:   Main issues in logistics networks in Swiss industry (Top 10)

The complete survey will be discussed in the following section.

2.3   Current state of transcorporate logistics in Swiss industry

Much has been written of late concerning the supplier-buyer relationship/co-makership[24], strategic supplier partnerships[25], and the broader notion of supply chain practices[26]. Several empirical studies have been conducted in the area of supply chain management. STUART investigated the predictors of alliance success and failures[27], SPEKMAN looked at the challenges involved when implementing SCM concepts[28] and NEW analyzed different types of customer-supplier relationships[29].

However, most surveys addressed just one side of the transcorporate relationship, either the supplier or customer side of a company, and only a few extended the investigation to examine matched buyer-supplier pairs[30]. The

---

[24]   MERLI, 1991.

[25]   FRIGO-MOSCA/ALBERTI, 1995.

[26]   MASON-JONES/TOWILL, 1997.

[27]   STUART, 1997.

[28]   SPEKMAN, 1998.

[29]   NEW/BURNES, 1997.

[30]   STUART, 1998.

survey presented here looks at three tiers of a supply chain simultaneously from the perspective of the surveyed company (suppliers – surveyed company – customers; see figure 2-9) to gather broader insights in the transcorporate logistics.

2.3.1 General objectives of the survey

In the survey, the current industrial practice of Swiss companies was investigated in the area of transcorporate logistics.[31] The fundamental purpose of the study was to examine the significance of supply chain activities, the spread of supply chain information technology, and the specific characteristic features of supply chain collaboration in Swiss companies. A further important question was how new information technology affects the development of transcorporate practice. The study also addressed the following issues in particular:

- What are the key issues and current practices in transcorporate logistics?

- How well does information technology currently support SCM activities and how do companies adapt to new information technology (e.g., the Internet, SCM software)?

- What are the key impacts of this new generation of information technology on collaboration and coordination in the transcorporate logistics?

2.3.2 Approach and sample of the survey

To find answers to these questions, a two-phase approach involving successive questionnaire mailings to companies in the process and discrete industries was taken. The first mailing was a one-page description of the survey on the scope, key objectives, industrial relevance, and target group. A fax answer sheet was included. The purpose of the mailing, which was addressed to company general management, was to gain company commitment to participate in the survey. The survey therefore mainly addressed general managers in SME who are quite familiar with their transcorporate relationships. In larger companies, general managers who did not feel knowledgeable enough to deal with the topic were asked to distribute the questionnaire to appropriate persons in their companies. This mailing also made it possible for us to personally address the subsequent questionnaire to individual people in management with access to the required information. As the base of this first round, a commercial address data base was used, which offered personalized addresses as well as numerous selection criteria related to the characteristics of the company (e.g., size, industry, region etc.).

---

[31] This survey was part of the research project ProNet funded by CTI 4674.1 KTS: State-of-the-art of Supply Chain Management Software – analysis of the needs of organizations and design guidelines for production networks with cooperation partners of Center for Enterprise Sciences (BWI-ETHZ), the Work and Organizational Psychology Unit (IFAP-ETHZ), ZPA of FH Aargau, and the Laboratoire de Gestion et Procédées de production (ICAP-EPFL).

The following table shows the selection criteria and the configuration of the sample.

Criteria of selection	Values
Company size	3 categories 11–50 employees 51–250 employees 251 and more employees
Industry sections (according to KOMPASS[32])	Discrete industry: electronics, automotive, textile, high-tech, metal, engineering, measuring and control technology. Process industry: pharmaceutical, chemical and paper industry.
Addressed employees	General Management
Location of company headquarters	Switzerland (German-speaking)

Table 1:   Criteria of selection

This selection resulted in 3741 addresses and, by comparing it with material from the Swiss Federal Statistical Office[33], it shows that for this type of companies, it is almost a complete count.

As mentioned, in the first round, we addressed 3741 general managers from a broad cross-section in Switzerland, SME as well as big global players. In this way, sample bias with regard to specific industries was avoided. The rebound response rate of this first round was around 6% (217 companies), which demonstrates high interest in the subject.

In the second round, the complete questionnaire consisting of the sections on supply chain activities and organization, supply chain information technology, and supply chain collaboration, with a total of 32 questions was sent out. Each respondent was asked questions about their perceptions of their external upstream and downstream counterparts in the supply chain. For example, general managers responded to questions about their key suppliers and their key customers, while procurement managers responded to questions about their key suppliers, and sales managers responded to questions about their key customers in the corresponding company. From these perspectives, an integral supply chain view of certain key dimensions of the logistics network could be obtained.

---

[32]   KOMPASS™ is a professional provider of address data bases with personalized addresses as well as numerous selection criteria for companies.

[33]   http://www.statistik.admin.ch/ (August 2001).

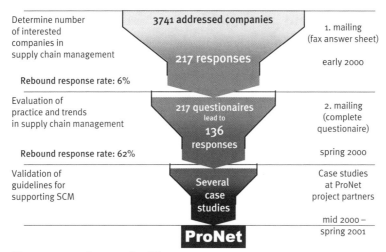

Figure 2-4:   Approach of the survey

The rebound response rate of this second round was 62%, which results in a sample base of n = 136 companies in Switzerland.

2.3.3   Design of the survey

The questionnaire was divided up into three sections and encompassed the following key aspects:

- *Questions related to the mechanism of coordination in the logistics network*

Here, the focus was on SCM tasks, which are heavily influenced by external relationships to customers as well as suppliers. The first part of the questionnaire was also mainly related to the SCM task reference model (see section 3.4.1). Companies were asked to rate the current state of their tasks involving transcorporate logistics and the areas they perceive as needing the most improvement.

- *Questions related to the information and communication technology (ICT) in use for transcorporate logistics*

In this section of the questionnaire, the current state of information technology in the companies was asked. The intention was to get to know how large the market penetration of IT support for transcorporate logistics (e.g., SCM software) in Switzerland currently is.

- *Questions related to the dimension of collaboration*

The largest part of the questionnaire related to the dimension of collaboration. Particularly, how collaborative behavior, according to the SCM paradigm, engages partners in joint planning, processes, and information sharing that go beyond the levels reached in less intense trading relationships.

2.3.4   Interviews and pretests

After designing the questionnaire, the relevance of the questions and the completeness were tested and improved by several interviews with experts[34]. The resulting reworked version was then (pre)tested by the ProNet project partner in order to prove the comprehensibility of the questions, the scope as well as a rough estimate about the amount of time needed for the data evaluation. These consolidated findings lead to some smaller changes and resulted in the final version of the questionnaire.

2.3.5   Collection of data and statistical evaluation

The returned questionnaires were all marked with an identification number and a variable with the corresponding values was allocated to every feature, based on a five digit nominal scale of 1–5 (1 connotes 'not at all' or 'unimportant', and 5 connotes 'to a very large extent'), which lead to 216 variables. The generated list of variables offers each possible answer to a question only one valid value, also called code, which was inserted then in the corresponding value field of the evaluation file. The evaluation of the questionnaire was done with the aid of the SPSS for Windows, Release 8.0.

The closed-loop questions were analyzed with a descriptive measured value by frequency, mean and standard deviation. The open questions were summarized context-analytically with the aid of a cluster analysis. For the graphical presentation, bar charts have been chosen. However, based on the small sample (n = 136), significance tests were only used for demonstration purposes. On the execution of further multi-variant analysis techniques was renounced. All the necessary statistical techniques for the evaluation of the underlying sample serve merely as descriptive presentation. The claim to a statistical reference sample in the narrow sense will not be raised, because the significant statistical dependence of the observed and expected frequencies could not be conducted with the chi-square-test[35] due to the small sample size of n = 136. However, by comparing the realized versus expected returns (compare table 2), the following general conclusion can be made.

Larger companies with 251 employees or more have participated more often in the survey, whereas smaller companies with 11 to 50 members participated less than expected compared to the sample population. One reason can be that this largest target group is less involved in these new logistics concepts, in comparison to larger companies, which are more advanced in this field (for instance – a main user of SCM software as survey results revealed). However, a

---

[34]   In this stage, the intensive knowledge of the IBM EMEA Global Services group, a member of the ProNet team, was included.

[35]   The chi-square test is used to test if a sample of data comes from a specific distribution or in other words, to test if the standard deviation of a observed sample significantly differs from a parent distribution (BOX ET AL., 1978, p. 89.).

targeted promotion by e-mail as well as telephone calls and a redesign of the survey that not only included questions, but explanations and definitions related to the research field as well, achieved a high second rebound rate of 62 %.[36]

Company size	Addressed companies (COMPASS)		Realized returns (valid questionnaires)		Expected returns (according to distribution of company size)	
	Amount	%	Amount	%	Amount	%
11–50	2015	57	55	41	77	(57)
51–100	788	22	35	26	30	(22)
101–250	481	14	29	21	19	(14)
251 and more	258	7	17	13	10	(7)
TOTAL	3542	100	136	100	136	100

Table 2:   Testing of statistical relevance

In conclusion, the result of the survey can be observed as an appropriate statistical reference cross section of the German-speaking Swiss industry landscape in the area of transcorporate logistics.

2.3.6   Survey results

Rather than presenting the full set of data for each section (standard deviations, min, max, t-tests, or p-values), only a sample of the most significant data is presented. For each question, some examples and description are given to narrow the interpretation possibilities. The following paragraph presents the six key findings[37]:

Key finding 1 – Importance of 'Network Planning' and Available-to-promise (ATP):

Companies most frequently mentioned customer order fulfillment management with its key task of the quick promising of an order delivery date, also known as available-to-promise (ATP) capability, as one of their core interests related to transcorporate logistics in the supply chain execution area. Furthermore, strategic enterprise planning (e.g., configuration and designing of the logistics network) and strategic sourcing and procurement received the next highest rankings as figure 2-5 depicts. This is a clear indication that most companies, as well as SME, have realized that integration into logistics networks is quite essential to their business success. On the tactical level (related to the task model in 3.4.1), demand and forecasting planning is ranked quite high. This

---

[36]   According to HAFERMALZ, statistical reference of a written survey is proved if the rebound rate is sufficiently high and all existing instrumental possibilities for reducing rebound failures were taken into account (HAFERMALZ, 1976, p. 191).

[37]   The full set of results of the survey have been published in HIEBER ET AL., 2000.

function relies particularly heavily on information from external customers, and for this reason, the results on information sharing practices in the next section are quite astonishing. The least important for companies are distribution planning and transportation planning.

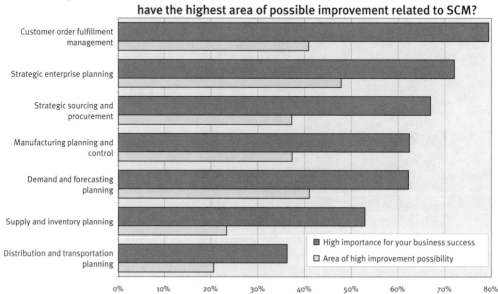

Figure 2-5:   Critical supply chain tasks and areas for improvement

In the same section, we also asked respondents about the areas requiring improvement. About 50% of the companies locate a very high to high potential for improvement in strategic enterprise planning. This underscores the importance of SCM concepts. Customer order fulfillment management received the next highest mention. Here, the affiliated business tasks, in particular, relate directly to customer satisfaction and therefore give an indication of company perceptions of the supply chain excellence based on their own customer service. Surprisingly, the areas with the lowest ratings in requiring improvement were supply and inventory planning and distribution and transportation planning because most of the currently available SCM software applications mainly address these tasks.

Key finding 2 – Concentration on core competence:

The outsourcing of logistics functions in the area of supply chain management is still very popular. Companies were asked about any parts of their 'internal' supply chains that are outsourced to date.

Question: Which logistics function are outsourced so far and what are you planning to do in this field?

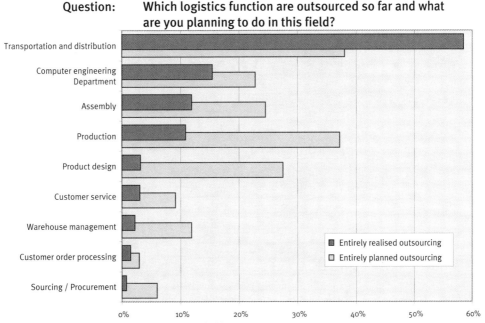

Figure 2-6:   Outsourcing activities

Distribution and transportation is clearly the main focus of outsourcing activities. Nowadays, over 60% of the companies have sourced out these functions. All other areas, like warehouse management, IT department, product development, or customer service are far behind. Furthermore, in the same question, planned outsourcing activities were also requested. Here, a significant level of outsourcing activities in production (close to 40%) as well as in product design could be seen. Transportation and distribution are still playing a leading role in further outsourcing activities with almost 40% as figure 2-6 depicts.

Key finding 3 – Satisfaction with IT support very limited:

In the next section of the questionnaire related to IT, with companies were asked what activities are currently supported by their information technology.

Question: **To what extent are you supported by IT and how satisfied are you with your IT support?**

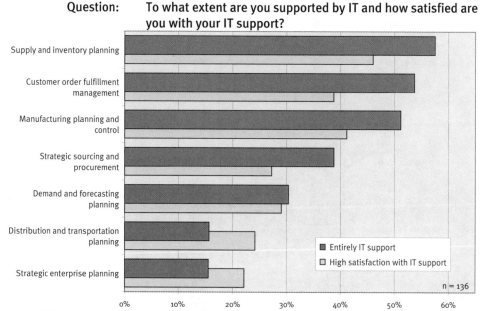

Figure 2-7:   IT support in logistics activities

Over 55% of the companies used the IT support entirely for supply and inventory planning, followed by customer order fulfillment management and manufacturing planning and control. These are basically the classic functions covered by ERP systems. More interesting are the companies' answers when asked about their levels of satisfaction with current IT support for these activities. The general level of satisfaction is quite low. Companies voiced the most satisfaction with IT support for supply and inventory planning, the traditional MRP function, followed by support for manufacturing planning and control and customer order fulfillment management. In general, the least supported business functions of today's companies, as well as the lowest IT satisfaction were observed in demand and forecast, distribution and transportation, and strategic planning. These functions are supported only to a small extent by the current ERP packages, however, more and more niche software vendors are addressing this area (e.g., i2 technologies, Manugistics, JDEdwards).

Key finding 4 – Traditional communication channels dominant:

Companies were next asked what kind of information and communication channels they use for information exchange with their main suppliers (volume >3% of total purchase) and with their main customers (volume >3% of total sales).

Question: **What kind of systems are in place to your suppliers and customers?**

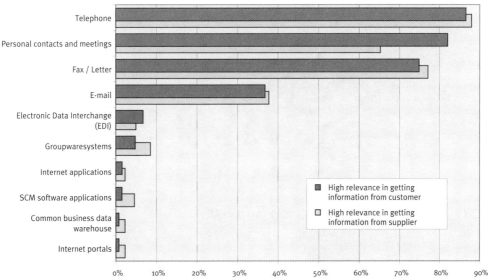

Figure 2-8:   Information and communication technology in use

The dominant channels for information sharing are still telephone calls and personal contacts. The use of advanced information technologies, such as SCM software applications or groupware systems, is negligible. In about 40% of the companies, e-mail has a high relevance in getting information from customer or supplier, but in contrast, its use is far behind the use of the fax (over 75%). Furthermore, companies believe that personal contacts with their customers are more important than with suppliers. On the supplier side, the dominant communication channel is still the telephone call, ahead of personal meetings and faxes.

Key finding 5 – Low level of information sharing:

Figures 2-10 and 2-11 show the current state of supply chain information sharing practices between the down- and upstream counterparts. In addition, figure 2-9 gives an indication of the directions of the information flow and the four possible 'platforms' of information exchange between a company and its suppliers, as well as customers, which had been taken into account in the survey.

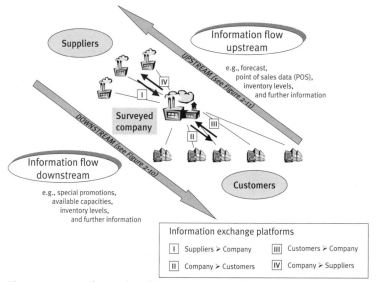

Figure 2-9:   Information flow upstream and downstream in the supply chain

Figure 2-10 reveals the information sharing practices from the key customers to the surveyed company and the further forwarding of logistics information to the key suppliers. In addition, a differentiation between soft and hard logistics facts has been made. Hard logistics facts are information that does not allow or has less interpretation scope and that are very meaningful and clear for the logisticians. This information should be forwarded ahead and processed for their own planning activities, e.g., inventory levels of the customers or forecast data. In contrast, soft logistics facts are numbers, which leave a lot of interpretation scope and cannot be used directly for further input for the company's own information processing system, such as early information about delivery problems.

As the results demonstrate in figure 2-10, the scope of information sharing, especially hard logistics information like inventory levels, capacity, order status and more, between the partners upstream of the supply chain is very low. The most commonly shared information is general information about new product releases or delivery problems, defined as soft logistics facts. The only small exception represents forecast data. Companies stated that they receive forecast numbers from around 20% of their key customers and furthermore, forward forecast information to over 30% of their key suppliers. The amount of shared information relevant to planning functions such as inventory levels, point of sales data, or production and assembly plans is insignificant.

Question: Information flow upstream in the supply chain

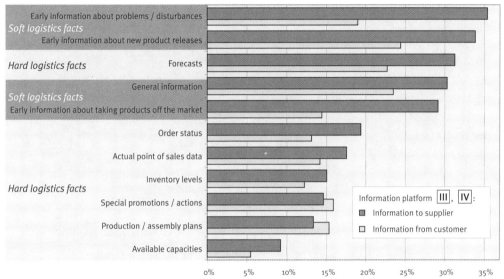

Figure 2-10:   Information sharing practice upstream in supply chain

Where the previous section examines what information flows upstream in the supply chain, this section examines what information flows downstream from the key suppliers to the surveyed company to the key customers in the supply chain. Surprisingly, information sharing intensity is twice as high here as in the upstream flow, but it is still at a very low level. Similarly, soft logistics facts are communicated most frequently rather than 'hard' logistics data, like inventory level, order status and more.

However, there are interesting similarities between the reported upstream and downstream flows. A strong impression can be gained that more information is shared to suppliers than is actually received from customers (demonstrated in both figures by the gap between the dark and light bars). Furthermore, these findings demonstrate that it is the companies' perception that they share and pass information to their partners, in this case their customers, to a much greater extent than they receive information from suppliers.

Question: Information flow downstream in the supply chain

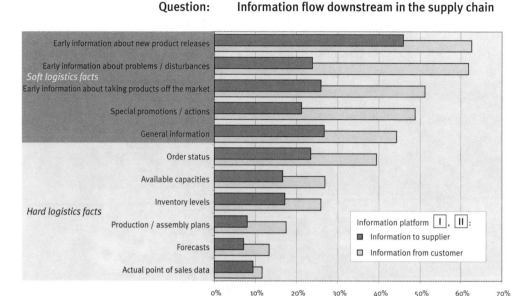

Figure 2-11:   Information sharing practice downstream in the supply chain

Key finding 6 – Improving information flow along the supply chain:

In the final section of the survey, the participants were asked to rate specific actions that could improve supply chain performance. Figure 2-12 summarizes the companies' ratings of an array of practices and actions for their supply chain improvement efforts. Information sharing between the partners is rated as the most efficient practice for the future business success by over 60%, followed by a better integration of the transcorporate planning and execution processes. In addition, 30% also rate the use of collaborative performance indicators as an appropriate improvement strategy with a high impact on business success. At the bottom of the list, the creation of a position of a supply chain manager is rated as the least important.

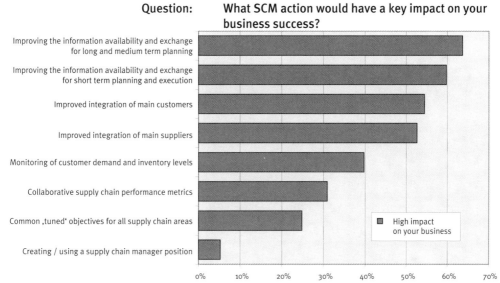

Figure 2-12:   Key actions to improve supply chain management

2.3.7   Conclusions of the survey

Although the benefits of information sharing are quite obvious, the results of the survey suggest that companies, especially SME, have put the concept of supply chain management into practice only to a very limited extent as yet. Furthermore, the answers show a clear discrepancy in the perception of the importance of information sharing and their implementation in daily business within the logistics network. In addition, it appears that the information flow downstream of the supply chain is greater than upstream (push versus pull of information). In general, in the companies' own perceptions, they give more information to their partners than they actually receive from their customers and suppliers. Furthermore, although companies often complain about excessive inventory, supply and inventory planning is not the major concern of companies so far today. On the contrary, most of the companies view integration into the supply chain and efficient information sharing as big opportunities for their future business success.

3

3 The state of the art of transcorporate logistics in industrial networks

In this section, basic definitions in the area of logistics will be discussed and will serve to clarify the scope of the discussed topics and presented concepts. In the field of logistics, as well as in transcorporate logistics, numerous definitions and different perceptions are in place (see section 3.1.4). In this book, the underlying definition of logistics is: An integral approach for the management of logistics systems for the design and manufacturing, service and use, and disposal of a product demanded by the final consumer or respectively the final marketplace (see figure 3-1).

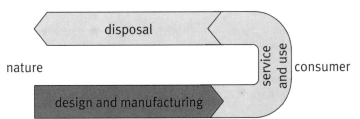

Figure 3-1:   Life cycle of a product supported by integral logistics management[38]

---

[38]   SCHÖNSLEBEN, 2000, p. 7.

3.1 Research fields and basic definitions in logistics

3.1.1 Logistics

Logistics management deals with the design and management of productive systems as well as with the planning and control of daily business operations within a company or in transcorporate networks.[39] Hence, logistics is involved with products over their entire life cycle (see figure 3-1).

Logistics in and among companies is the organization, planning, and realization of the total flow of goods, data, and control along the entire life cycle of products (SCHÖNSLEBEN, 2000).[40]

The concept of logistics originated in military discipline, but logistics in management science has few links to military logistics. No universal definition of logistics exists in the literature, but the definition sometimes referred to as the simplified LAYMAN's description of logistics, which has appeared in many definitions, is the so-called **7 Rs**: To ensure the availability of the right product, in the right quantity, and in the right condition, at the right place, at the right time, for the right customer, at the right cost. The underline of emphasis on availability is not the usual emphasis, but this definition expresses, without being very specific, the core functions of logistics.

3.1.2 Logistics network

For the purpose of this work, logistics network is used as a synonym for supply chains because this term points out more clearly the fact that several partners are interconnected to each other within a network of relationships. Logistics networks are defined as follows:

A logistics network is a network of entities through which material and information flow, encompassing all related activities associated with the flow and transformation of goods in the respective area of the network. Those entities may include suppliers, carriers, manufacturing sites, distribution centers, retailers, information brokers (e.g., SCM managers) up to the final customers.

3.1.3 Supply chain management

Supply chain management (SCM) is the integration of the activities associated with the flow and transformation of goods in the respective logistics networks through improved supply chain relationships based on a common collaborative

---

[39]   SCHÖNSLEBEN, 2000, p. 3.

[40]   SCHÖNSLEBEN, 2000, p. 7.

performance measurement framework for attaining close, collaborative and well-coordinated network relationships to achieve a sustainable competitive advantage.

SCHÖNSLEBEN stresses the feature of an underlying long-term, strategic relationship and enlarges the definition with elements of collaborative product design and defines SCM as the coordination of strategic and long-term cooperation among co-makers in the total logistics network for the development and production of products, both in production and procurement and in product and process innovation. Each co-maker is active within his own area of core competence. The choice of co-maker is made with chief importance according to its potential towards realization of short lead times.[41]

According to the APICS dictionary[42], *supply* is the quantity of goods available for use as well as the actual or planned replenishment of a product or component. The replenishment quantities are created in response to a demand for the product or component or in anticipation of such a demand. *Supply chain* is the process from the initial raw materials to the ultimate consumption of the finished product linked across supplier-user companies as well as the functions inside and outside a company that enable the value chain to make products and provide services to the customer. Finally, *supply chain management* is the planning, organizing, and controlling of supply chain activities. In general, supply chain management is redefined as a process of designing, developing, optimizing, and managing the external as well as internal components of a supply chain system. This includes material supply, transforming materials, and distributing finished goods or services to the end consumer.[43] A very often used and appropriate graphic representation for the basic underlying concept is provided by the SCOR model. Figure 3-2 shows the structure of a simple multi-stage supply chain (for more detail, see sections 3.4.2 and 5.2.2).

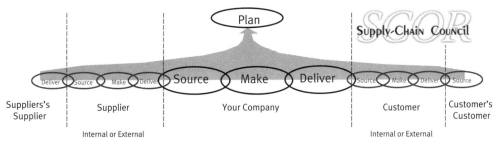

Figure 3-2:   SCOR model level 1

Based on the SCOR model, a supply chain is simply a network of several chains of material processing cells called source, make, deliver and associated planning activities. Please note that the example in figure 3-2 shows a very simple one-to-

---

[41]   SCHÖNSLEBEN, 2000, p. 54.

[42]   APICS 1998, p. 93.

[43]   SPEKMAN ET AL. 1998.

one linear structure. In reality, goods flows diverge and converge, which makes supply chain management much more complex and difficult to manage.

3.1.4   Synopsis of supply chain management definitions

Supply chain management is a relatively new concept in the research literature and still lacks a clear definition among academics and industry professionals. The first papers related to SCM appeared in the early eighties. Among them were a dozen similar papers from the consultants BOOZ, ALLEN & HAMILTON, which contained the following basic underlying concept:

"Supply chain management as a new logistics concept differs significantly from classical materials and manufacturing control in this respect: It views the supply chain as a single entity rather than relegating fragmented responsibility for various segments in the chain."[44]

The following synopsis of SCM definitions will try to demonstrate the key elements and essential components, which can be found in the research literature. However, while many definitions of SCM exist, the objective is not to select the best and latest definition, but rather to show the different points of view.

BECHTEL and JAYARAM have developed a classification structure for the numerous different SCM theories and definitions, and the results are presented in the following framework, the so-called four *Supply Chain Schools of Thought*[45]. Furthermore, not only the different points of use in SCM, but also the timely development combined with the enhancement in scope and content can be followed.

---

[44]   KEITH OLIVER/WEBBER, 1982, p. 63.

[45]   BECHTEL/JAYARAM, 1997, p. 15.

Author(s)	Definition of Supply Chain Management
Chain Awareness School	
Jones/Riley[46] (1985)	"Supply Chain Management deals with the total flow of materials from suppliers through end users."
Houlihan[47] (1985)	"Supply Chain Management covers the flow of goods from supplier through manufacturing and distribution chains to the end user."
Stevens[48] (1989)	"Controls the flow of material from suppliers, through the value-adding (production) processes and distribution channels, to customers."
Lee/Billington[49] (1992)	"Networks of manufacturing and distribution sites that procure raw materials, transform them into intermediate and finished products, and distribute the finished products to consumers."
Linkage School	
Scott/West-brook[50] (1991)	"... supply chain is used to refer to the chain linking each element of the production and supply process from raw material through to the end customer."
Turner[51] (1993)	"... technique that looks at all the links in the chain from raw materials suppliers through various levels of manufacturing to warehousing and distribution to the final customer."
Information School	
Johannson[52] (1994)	"Supply Chain Management is really an operations approach to procurement. It requires all participants of the supply chain to be properly informed. With SCM, the linkage and information flow between various members of the supply chain are critical to overall performance."
Towill[53] (1997)	"A supply chain is a system, the constituent parts of which include material suppliers, production facilities, distribution services, customers linked together via the feed forward of materials and the feedback flow of information."
Harrington[54] (1995)	"Production and information flow encompassing all parties beginning with the supplier's suppliers and ending with customers or consumers/end users ... flows are bidirectional."

Table 3:   Synopsis of supply chain management definitions (I/II)

---

[46]   JONES/RILEY, 1985, p. 16.
[47]   HOULIHAN, 1985, p. 26.
[48]   STEVENS, 1989, p. 3.
[49]   LEE/BILLINGTON, 1992, p. 65.
[50]   SCOTT/WESTBROOK 1991, p. 23.
[51]   TURNER, 1993, p. 52.
[52]   JOHANNSON, 1994, p. 521.
[53]   TOWILL, 1997, p. 37.
[54]   HARRINGTON, 1995, p. 30.

Author(s)	Definition of Supply Chain Management
Integration School	
Cooper/Ellram[55] (1990)	"An integrative philosophy to manage the total flow of a distribution channel from the supplier to the ultimate user."
Ellram[56] (1991)	"Supply Chain Management is an integrative approach to using information to manage the materials flow from suppliers to end-user to achieve improved customer service at reduced overall costs, SCM represents a network of firms interacting to deliver a product or service to the end customer."
Hewitt[57] (1994)	"Supply chain integration is only a natural result of redesigned business processes not realignment of existing functional organization."

Table 4:   Synopsis of supply chain management definitions (II/II)

Based on the research of BECHTEL AND JAYARAM[58], most of the existing definitions in supply chain management can be divided into the following four categories:

- *The Functional Chain Awareness School*

The functional chain awareness school of thought recognizes the existence of a chain of functional areas. Most of the definitions conclude that the supply chain encompasses all the material flows from the suppliers to the final customer. Important is the fact that all members of the value-adding process – from the raw materials up to consumption – are embedded in these definitions. However, the main focus is merely the physical material flow, which reflects the origin of these definitions from the traditional field of logistics.

- *The Linkage School*

In the definitions of the linkage school, the focus is on the interfaces between the different entities in the supply chain. A good way to distinguish between the chain awareness and linkage school is to realize that in the awareness school, the supply chain is simply a chain of different functions – e.g., purchasing, production, distribution, warehousing – which should be managed (simultaneously) – the linkage school begins to investigate how linkages among the functional areas can be exploited for competitive advantages. The emphasis is on smoothing the flow of material between the partners to reduce inventory.

- *The Information School*

The information school focuses on the information flow between the partners. Not only the flow from customers to suppliers (unidirectional), but also information from the suppliers to the customers have to be taken into account (bi-directional – see also survey results in section 2.3.6). All members should have access to all relevant information they need for their logistics purpose.

---

[55] COOPER/ELLRAM 1990, p. 1.

[56] ELLRAM, 1991, p. 17.

[57] HEWITT, 1994, p. 2.

[58] BECHTEL/JAYARAM 1997, pp. 16–18.

Based on these definitions, information is the backbone of effective supply chain management.

- *The Integration/Process School*

The integration school, with the most recent and advanced definitions, focuses on integrating supply chain areas into a system defined as a set of processes that adds value to the customer. The biggest changes to the previous perception of SCM is that the focus is on customer satisfaction regardless of the configuration of the functional areas in the supply chain, in contrast to the previous understanding of gaining as much efficiency as possible from this sequence of functions.

This categorization is a very suitable approach for classifying different types of SCM definitions. Although not all existing definitions can be mentioned, it is a helpful device and good starting point for clarifying the various SCM definitions. Most of other existing definitions can easily be mapped and added to these four areas. However, in recent definitions and the most advanced SCM understanding, a further dimension can be identified that stresses the collaborative and win-win partnership orientation in SCM: *collaboration school*[59], see section 3.2.4.

3.2   Development of logistics from a single function towards a network orientation

This chapter seeks to explore the various evolution theories that mark the development of modern logistics management, culminating in the emergence of the supply chain management strategy. Several perspectives on logistics development can be identified. Following this discussion, the final part of this chapter combines the various elements and demonstrates the evolution of logistics towards an integrated approach.

3.2.1   A management perspective: the four management stages

According to Ross, logistics can be seen as evolving through four distinct areas: warehousing and transportation management, total cost management, integrated logistics management and supply chain management (see table 5).

In the first management stage, logistics was perceived purely as a tactical function consisting of a decentralized group of enterprise operational activities associated primarily with warehousing and transportation. The second stage of logistics can be characterized as the conscious centralization of logistics functions targeted at optimizing operation costs and customer service. The third stage is composed of two management concepts. The first can be described as the integration of core logistics functions with inventory planning, order

---

[59]   REINHART ET AL., 2001, p. 36.

processing, production planning, and purchasing. The second concept can be found in the extension of logistics interaction outside the company to embrace the entire supply channel, beginning with the supplier and concluding with the delivery to the customer.

Period	Stage 1 to 1960s	Stage 2 1970s–1980s	Stage 3 1980s–1990s	Stage 4 1990s–2000s
Management stage	Warehousing and trans-portation	Total cost management	Integrated logistics management	Supply chain management
Management focus	Operations performance	Optimizing operations, cost & custo-mer service	Tactics/ strategies, logistics planning	Supply chain visions, objectives & goals
Organization design	Decentralized functions	Centralized functions	Integration of logistics functions	Partnering, 'virtual' organization, market co-evolution

Table 5:   The four management stages in supply chain management[60]

The fourth, and final stage of logistics can be found in the emergence of SCM.[61] According to Ross' model, at the core of phase 4, SCM is defined as having two dimensions and centers on organizations with which to form close relationships with channel partners. The first dimension consists of an operational strategy based on accelerating the cycle times of inventory and information flow and optimizing the linkages between internal functions and supply partners. The second consists of the continuous networking of the competencies of intersecting supply channels focused around the creation of shared marketplace and competition visions. Ross is also one of the first authors who pinpoints the fact that the first and most important of the SCM strategic resources are the people who define the company's work culture and plan and execute the enterprise business functions. This is demonstrated in figure 3-4, where the degree of SCM perception is the most advanced.

---

[60]   Ross 1997, p. 78.
[61]   Ross, 1997, pp. 72–107.

3.2.2   An industrial environmental perspective: logistics in retrospective

Another simplified explanation of the developments of logistics is given by MOELLER. He states that the advancement in logistics has emerged as a consequence of the changing industrial environment throughout time.[62]

In the 1950s, core interest was production volumes and at this time, production was excluded from *logistics*. Logistics was mainly related to inventory movements. Increased service and more diversified products were the 60s trends in the market. Inventory was, at that time, the prevailing mechanism between supply and demand. The efficient physical distribution, warehousing and material handling were observed as logistics activities. The change from growth to stagnation was the profile of the 70s. Logistical costs increased and the cost of capital exploded as well. Inventory turnover rates were the main focus, and logistics was seen from a holistic system's perspective (including production). In the 80s, a revolution in information technology had a significant influence on logistics. Computer integrated manufacturing (CIM) was the major buzzword. Sales, purchasing and further administration functions were combined with production and distribution functions by integrated information systems (e.g., SAP R/3) and the trends towards Japanese manufacturing concepts, like JIT and total quality management in every aspect (TQM), was everywhere apparent.

Time period	Industrial environment	Industry focus	Logistics focus
50s	Unsaturated markets, Production volume	Costs	Inventories
60s	Increased service and more diversified products	Service	Distribution
70s	Capital deployment	Profitability	Production
80s	Competition, saturated markets	Total Quality Management	Purchase, production, sales
90s	Globalization, partnership, ecology	Time	Business processes

Table 6:   *Changes in the industrial environment related to logistics*[63]

In the 90s, themes like global manufacturing, alliances and ecology appeared, which have to be dealt with by even small and medium-sized companies. Time is emphasized as the single most important factor in logistics. As a consequence, many companies have been forced into order production – from a make-to-stock environment towards an assembly/make-to-order, one-of-a-kind production or

---

[62]   MOELLER, 1995, pp. 25–27.

[63]   MOELLER, 1995, p. 30.

even engineer-to-order. As a result of the changing industrial environment and the new resulting logistics requirements, the logistics focus steadily changed from inventories to business processes. In table 6, some of the important developments are summarized.

3.2.3   An integration perspective: the integrated supply chain

CHRISTOPHER states that the concept of supply chain management is in fact no more than an extension of the logic of logistics. As a matter of fact, in the traditional perception, logistics management is primarily concerned with optimizing flows within the organization while supply chain management recognizes that internal integration by itself is not sufficient.[64]

Therefore, STEVENS suggests a four stage integration model (see figure 3-3).

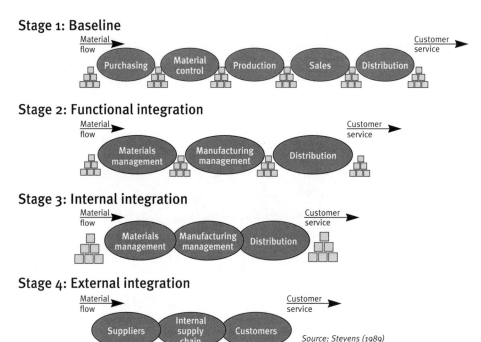

Stage 1: Baseline

Material flow · Purchasing · Material control · Production · Sales · Distribution · Customer service

Stage 2: Functional integration

Material flow · Materials management · Manufacturing management · Distribution · Customer service

Stage 3: Internal integration

Material flow · Materials management · Manufacturing management · Distribution · Customer service

Stage 4: External integration

Material flow · Suppliers · Internal supply chain · Customers · Customer service

Source: Stevens (1989)

Figure 3-3:   Integration of logistics functions by Stevens

STEVENS provides a framework for achieving an integrated supply chain[65]. Figure 3-3 suggests that there is in effect an evolution of integration from the stage 1 position of complete functional independence where each business function such as production or purchasing is responsible for their own activities and hence isolated optimization is the result. In this stage, most supply chains are

---

[64]   CHRISTOPHER, 1998, p. 16.

[65]   STEVENS, 1989, p. 6.

fragmented and are characterized by staged inventories, independent and often incompatible control systems and mostly heavy organizational boundaries.

Stage 2 of development involves functional integration, which focuses principally on the inward flow of goods. This means that companies have recognized the need for at least a limited degree of integration between adjacent functions, e.g., distribution and inventory management. Main characteristics here are still the emphasis on cost reduction rather than performance improvement. Customer orders are aggregated and forwarded and as a result, there is poor visibility of real customer demand, which leads to inadequate planning and excessive buffer stocks between the different units.

In stage 3, the establishment and implementation of an 'end-to-end' planning framework within the company is in place. Related to the planning and control systems, companies will use integrated ERP systems, including combined DRP and well-managed master schedules to an MRP/APS system. This stage involves the integration of those aspects of the supply chain directly under the control of the individual company.

In stage 4, full supply chain integration is achieved by extending the scope of integration outside the company in that the concept of linkage and coordination is now extended upstream to suppliers and downstream to customers.

3.2.4   Discussion of SCM definitions and conclusions

Recent definitions exist that broaden the research focus from operational to a more strategic perspective. In the future, the two following aspects will more and more influence the predominant understanding of the concept of supply chain management.

On one side, the concept for SCM will be more and more closely tied to the concepts of partnerships, strategic alliances, and risk and reward sharing strategies between network partners. Therefore, a greater emphasis is placed on the strategic and relational as opposed to the current predominant transactional view involved in SCM, as the previous description of the different evolution concepts and definitions has revealed. This development is shown in figure 3-4, where the different evolution stages are embedded – from the purely physical material flow to information sharing and integrated management concepts towards a more strategic and partnership orientation. This development is combined with an enhancement of the content and scope of the participating network functions and units, as figure 3-4 demonstrates. This will also lead to the situation that from stage 2 on, 'external' supply chain management will be the key perspective, rather than most of the current 'internal' SCM orientation.

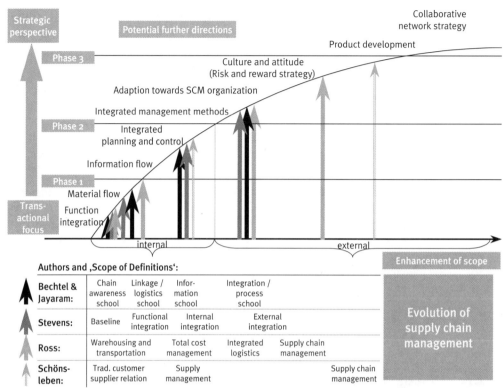

Figure 3-4:   *Key elements and development of the SCM paradigm*

The second major shift in definition elements in SCM is that the customer and final consumer will get more and more attention. It is not appropriate to start at the supply side. The term supply chain suggests that supply begins and drives the chain of activities. However, any chain must begin with a customer who demands a service or product. Hence, the idea of demand chain management is already the new buzzword.[66]

Some interesting aspects concerning the term 'supply chain management' can also be found in PFOHL. He demonstrates the limitation of the current SCM definitions and their associated weakness – the use of the term 'chain' and the related linear, (over)simplified view. Issues that arise because companies are usually not part of just one supply chain, but can be integrated into various chains with different logistics requirements at the same time are not sufficiently addressed[67]. Therefore, in this work, the term logistics network will mainly be used. However, the final definition of SCM and its elements have still not been determined yet.

---

[66]   E.g., see keynote speech of Prof. Eero Eloranta at the IFIP WG5.7 International Conference on Advances in Production Management Systems, September 6–10, 1999, Berlin.

[67]   PFOHL, 2000, p. 389.

3.3   Further theories of evolution of cooperations and networks

There is a long history for the evolution theory of cooperation in many fields of fundamental research, for example, economics, psychology, sociology, political science, and mathematics. Most of the time, the main question to be answered is when should an individual, organization or nation cooperate, and "when should a 'unit' be selfish in an ongoing interaction with another 'unit'". In other words, "under what conditions will co-operation emerge in a world of egoists without central authorities"[68].

Several theories of explanation of the phenomenon of cooperation exist. In the following, the most popular and relevant theories for this work will be explained briefly.

3.3.1   Transaction cost theory

The most popular theory of explanation for the evolution of cooperation is given by Ronald Coase[69]. His theory is based on classical cost arguments published in the "Theory of the Firm". Transaction costs refer to the costs of providing for some good or service through the market rather than having it provided from within the firm, and are mainly related to friction when passing over to the next stage[70]. Coase describes the transaction costs he is concerned with in his article:

"In order to carry out a market transaction it is necessary to discover who it is that one wishes to deal with, to conduct negotiations leading up to a bargain, to draw up the contract, to undertake the inspection needed to make sure that the terms of the contract are being observed, and so on."[71]

More succinctly, transaction costs are search and information costs, bargaining and decision costs, policing and enforcement costs. Coase contends that without taking transaction costs into account, it is impossible to understand properly the working of the economic system or have a sound basis for establishing economic policy. Coase observes that market prices govern the relationships between firms, but within a firm decisions are made on a basis different from maximizing profit subject to market prices. Within the firm, decisions are made through entrepreneurial coordination. The unsuitability of short-term contracts arises from the costs of collecting information and the costs of negotiating contracts. This leads to long-term contracts in which the remuneration is specified for the contractee in return for obeying, within limits, the direction of the entrepreneur.

---

[68]   Axelrod, 1984, p. 3.

[69]   Noble prize winner Ronald H. Coase; this fundamental work was actually written in 1937 – see Coase, R.H., 'The nature of the firm', In: *Economica*: 4, 1937, pp. 386–405.

[70]   Williamson, 1985, p. 1.

[71]   Coase, 1988, p. 6.

As opposed to neoclassical economic theory, where market works by price signal without costs, transaction cost theory presupposes the costs associated with transactions. In other words, the search for information regarding the possibilities for exchange and the negotiation and arrangement of the details of exchange (e.g., with respect to price, quantity, quality, insurance, transportation, timing and the preparation of documents, including legal contracts) involves expenditures of time and money[72]. The most important adaptation to the existence of transaction costs is the emergence of the firm. The fact that it costs something to enter into these transactions means that firms will emerge to organize what would otherwise be market transactions whenever their costs are less than the costs of carrying out the transactions through the market.

Although this theorem has its limitation in the field of logistics management, for instance, a lack of flexibility costs and the costs of lead time[73], it is a simple, suitable approach that explains the evolution of industrial networks related to outsourcing activities. As soon as the transaction costs, e.g., friction loss through the coordination of relations between company decreases, there is a good opportunity to broaden external cooperation by forming an industrial logistics network.

3.3.2   Principal-agent theory

Principal-agent (P-A) analysis has emerged as a popular and useful tool in the social sciences since the early 1970s, especially in accounting, finance, economics, management and organization theory. A principal-agent relationship has arisen between two (or more) parties when one, designated as the agent, acts for, on behalf of, or as representative for the other, designated the principal, in a particular domain of decision problems[74]. Hereby, the agent is empowered to act for the principal because the principal chooses to hire the agent or because there is an implicit contract between principal and agent. The P-A problem lies in the fact that differences of interest and information between the two parties mean that the agent may not always act in the interests of the principal, and the costs and difficulties of selecting an agent and monitoring his performance mean that the principal may not be able to enforce his will on the agent. The central dilemma investigated by principal-agent theorists is how to get the employee or contractor (agent) to act in the best interests of the principal (the employer) when the employee or contractor has an informational advantage over the principal and has different interests from the principal.

Typical P-A interactions mentioned in the literature include those in the commercial-economic-managerial realm (e.g., shareholders and company managers, managers and employees, landlords and sharecroppers, clients and

---

[72]   WILLIAMSON, 1991, p. 90.

[73]   SCHÖNSLEBEN, 2000, p. 41.

[74]   ROSS, 1973, p. 134.

professionals, insurance companies and policy holders) and is, based on its universality approach, partly transferable to network organizations.[75]

3.3.3   Prisoner's dilemma theory

The most depicted theory of explanation of the evolution of cooperation is the *Prisoner's dilemma*[76] approach with its underlying game theory. The game allows the players to achieve mutual gains from cooperation, but it also allows for the possibility that one player will exploit the other, or the possibility neither will cooperate.[77] The key question in this particular situation is how can cooperation ever develop in situations where each individual has an incentive to be selfish (compare figure 3-5, e.g., it pays to defect if you think the other player will cooperate).

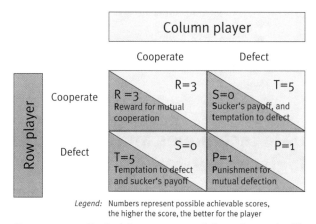

Legend: Numbers represent possible achievable scores, the higher the score, the better for the player

Figure 3-5:   Underlying concept of the prisoner's dilemma

Several research efforts have proven that if you play several rounds of the game and communication is allowed between the players, a long-term profit maximization will be feasible through cooperation[78]. However, non-cooperation models are also possible. Under this conditions, the most suitable strategy is the *tit for tat*-strategy[79], which means that each player starts with a co-operative strategy on the first move and then does whatever the other player did on his previous move.

---

[75]   SYDOW, 1999, pp. 279 and BALLING, 1997.

[76]   The Prisoner's Dilemma game was invented in about 1950 by MERILL FLOOD AND MELVIN DRESHER, and formalized by A.W. TUCKER shortly thereafter (see AXELROD, 1984, p. 216).

[77]   AXELROD, 1984, p. 7.

[78]   RÜDIGER, 1998, pp. 35.

[79]   This strategy was developed and proven by the game theorist and psychologist Anatol Rapoport of the University of Toronto in 1980. For the entire results, see *Axelrod, R. "Effective Choice in the Prisoners's Dilemma", Journal of Conflict Resolution, 1980, pp. 24:3–25.*

3.3.4   Conclusions to the theories of 'evolution of cooperation'

In research, there is a *lack of an overarching cooperation theory* that is suitable for the explanation of the different transcorporate types of cooperation. SYDOW states that merely one approach is hardly sufficient to explain the numerous forms and interdependencies.[80] He suggests that by using various theoretical approaches, it would guarantee that all dimensions would be revealed and best understood.

However, in logistics networks, some limitations and restrictions apply to the current theory approaches. In most of the considerations, the influence of power, interdependence, trust, social structures between the partners and entrepreneurial flexibility is particularly neglected. In addition, PICOT criticized that the theories do not consider whether the business is related to the core competence or is only considered a support function. Furthermore, it only distinguishes between the extremes of make or buy and no option in-between is valid.[81]

Therefore, these explanations are not quite transferable to the theory of the evolution of collaboration in logistics networks, they but have still value in the fundamental basic approach.

3.4   Transcorporate techniques and concepts for industrial logistics networks

In the following section, the most common and popular techniques and concepts in the area of supply chain management will be presented. Not only the most common organizational concepts will be highlighted, but also the new developments in information technology as well.

3.4.1   Task reference model for transcorporate logistics

Another way to describe transcorporate logistics is by means of tasks and functions (see figure 3-6). Three main categories of tasks can be distinguished – tasks related to supply chain design, supply chain planning and supply chain execution, which are related to operational, tactical, and strategic levels.

At the strategic level, the main focus is on the configuration and modeling of the supply chain network over the long term, the so-called strategic network design tasks. Moreover, scenarios of different warehouse locations, alternative distribution and supply channels, new production facilities and capacities must be taken into consideration and evaluated within this task group. The output of these

---

[80]   SYDOW, 1992, pp. 9.

[81]   PICOT, 1993, p. 184.

business tasks are solutions for an optimized design and configuration of the logistics network structure.

On the tactical level, the objective is to allocate resources (materials, capacities) to the expected and forecasted demand along the entire supply chain in a cost-efficient way for the long- to mid-term timeframe. Here the array of planning tasks comprises demand planning, supply network planning, supply, production, and distribution planning. These tasks rely heavily on information from counterparts in the supply chain and are currently mainly supported in isolation by each partner's traditional enterprise resource planning (ERP) system.[82] Hence, the output, mainly rough plans and master schedules for the respective network entities, will serve as input for the local corporate operational level.

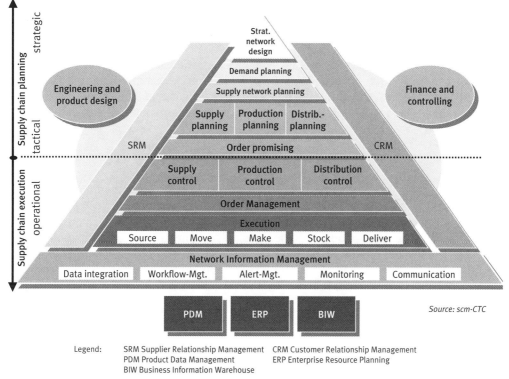

Legend: SRM Supplier Relationship Management   CRM Customer Relationship Management
            PDM Product Data Management   ERP Enterprise Resource Planning
            BIW Business Information Warehouse

Figure 3-6:   Task reference model of transcorporate logistics

On the operational level, the execution, especially customer order management with related local planning and control functions, is the focal point, which is triggered by planned or actual demand within a part of the network. At this level, the main concern in transcorporate logistics is the communication of real-time information between the partners. Here, the order promising task plays a special role. This task is the interface between the tactical planning and the execution,

---

[82]   HIEBER/ALARD, 2000, p. 683.

also known as available- or capable-to-promise task, which checks the availability (ATP) of finished goods, components or resources. In general, order promising commits order quantities based on actual stocks, plans and allocations.

3.4.2   The supply chain operation reference model (SCOR)

The SCOR model (Supply Chain Operations Reference Model) is a business process reference model, which has been developed by the Supply Chain Council (SCC)[83], an independent not-for-profit corporation. The model claims to link process elements, metrics, best practice and the features associated with the planning and execution of a supply chain. Therefore, the SCOR model consists of a descriptive process framework, with a standard glossary of terms (latest version 4.0, summer 2001, since the Model's introduction in 1996) and has been endorsed as the cross-industry standard for supply chain management.

The main objective of the SCOR model is to provide a common language for communication among supply chain partners by describing the business activities associated with all phases of satisfying customer demand.[84] Therefore, the SCOR model is founded on four distinct management processes:

- *Plan*
- *Source*
- *Make*
- *Deliver*

It also includes the logistics performance indicators related to each process step. The scope of the model encompasses all customer interactions from order entry through paid invoices, all physical material transactions including equipment, suppliers, spare parts, bulk product, and software, and all market interactions from the understanding of aggregate demand to the fulfillment of each order.[85]

The model itself is organized around a four level top-down approach, whereby the first three levels are supported by SCOR and level four is company specific (see figure 3-7).

---

[83]   The SCC was founded in 1996 by PITTIGLIO RABIN TODD & McGRATH (PRTM) and AMR Research, and initially included 69 voluntary member companies. Council membership is now open to all companies and organizations interested in applying and advancing state-of-the-art supply chain management systems and practices and now encompasses around 800 members (March 2001). For more information, visit the Web site: www.supply-chain.org (August 2001).

[84]   SCOR model, 2000, Version 4.0, p. 2.

[85]   SCOR model 2000, Version 3.1.

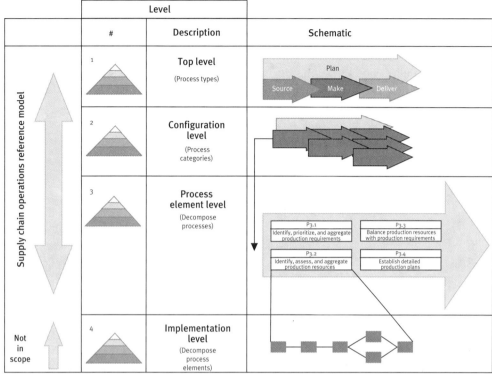

Figure 3-7:   SCOR as a hierarchical approach

In the following, SCOR Version 3.1 will be discussed in more detail, because the new SCOR model version 4.0 is still in its consolidation stage at present. However, major changes will be highlighted at the end of this section.

Level 1 defines the scope and content for the supply chain operations reference model, the four basic management processes. Here, the basis of the competition performance targets are set. At level 2, a company's supply chain can be 'configured-to-order' from twenty-four reference core process categories.[86] Companies implement their operations strategy through the configuration they choose for their supply chain. At level 3, the configured processes were decomposed and specified by the associated process elements. Here, companies can 'fine tune' their operations strategy. Level 3 consists of process element definitions, process element information input, and output, process performance metrics, best practices and system capabilities required to support best practices, including software applications where applicable.[87] At level 4, each company has to define their own specific management practices.

---

[86]   24 process categories in version 3.1, extended in version 4.0 to 26 process categories.

[87]   SCOR model 4.0, p. 6.

The model at level 2, which is the core of the toolkit[88], is described in the following section in more detail with the respective elements. Figure 3-8 shows the basic level 2 structure. The model itself contains several sections and is organized around the four primary management processes of plan, source, make, and deliver and the supporting enabling elements. Altogether, using twenty-four reference process categories with best practices, benchmarking data[89] and software functionality, the supply chain can be configured.

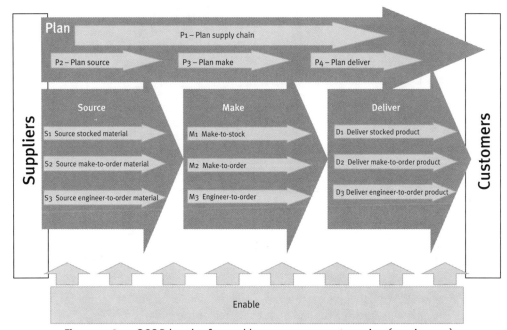

Figure 3-8:   SCOR level 2 formed by 24 process categories (version 3.1)

In general, the management processes[90] can be defined as follows:

- *Plan* – processes that balance aggregated demand and supply to develop a course of action that best meets sourcing, production and delivery requirements.

- *Source* – processes that procure goods and services to meet planned or actual demand.

- *Make* – processes that transform products to a finished state to meet planned or actual demand.

---

[88]   In addition, in chapter 6, the model will be enhanced with collaboration planning elements.

[89]   Best Practices were collected over numerous branches and are made available to members who are willing to commit to participating in a benchmark study.

[90]   SCOR model, Version 4.0, p. 7.

- *Deliver* – processes that provide finished goods and services to meet planned or actual demand, typically including order management, transportation management, and distribution management.

- *Return* – processes associated with the return of products for any reason and extending into post-delivery customer support (new in version 4.0).

As figure 3-8 demonstrates, by describing supply chains using these process building blocks, it should be possible to generate a common, comparable and ratable process model of supply chains.

As mentioned at the beginning, SCOR supports the communication between partners in a supply chain very well through a common language. However, as will be discussed in more detail in section 5.2.2, it does not cover the business interactions and associated performance attributes among network partners in a transcorporate perspective, and is therefore mainly an inter-corporate approach[91].

3.4.3   Advanced logistic partnership model (ALP)

The key idea of the advanced logistic partnership (ALP) model is to optimize the entire logistics chain, starting with the raw material up to the end user product, thus increasing the competitiveness of all the members of the chain.[92] Therefore, the ALP makes a claim for a new partnership culture by providing a reference model, which is built upon around three management levels:

- *executive management*

- *senior management*

- *operational management*

In addition, three different phases in the relationship between suppliers and customers are identified:

- *intention*

- *definition*

- *execution*

As a result, the model spans a 3x3 matrix with a total of nine quadrants. Most significantly, achieving a win-win situation is the guiding principle within the *advanced logistic partnership* model[93], which puts this basic principle into concrete terms by providing instruments and techniques to support the supply chain activities for each quadrant. For instance, at the executive management level, general guidelines for the interactions serve to build trust and to establish

---

[91]   Supply Chain Council minutes, PLAN Technical Committee meeting, January 2001, p. 2.

[92]   FRIGO-MOSCA/ALBERTI, 1995, pp. 31–35.

[93]   The ALP model was developed at the Center for Enterprise Sciences (BWI) of the Swiss Federal Institute of Technology (FTH) in Zurich and is discussed in detail in SCHÖNSLEBEN 2000.

principal legal relationships are stated, at the senior management level, the collaborative development of products and processes are discussed and, at the operational management level, ways of order processing are presented. Furthermore, by distinguishing among the three phases in the relationship between suppliers and customers – the intention phase with choices of potential partners, the definition phase with exploration of possible solutions and basic decision making, and finally the execution phase with operations and continuous improvements – the primary sequence of forming and operating a logistics network is recommended, which is also marked throughout the matrix by the arrows in figure 3-9[94].

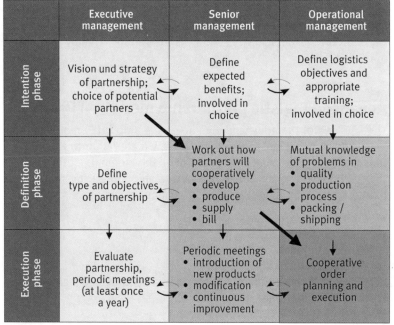

	Executive management	Senior management	Operational management
Intention phase	Vision und strategy of partnership; choice of potential partners	Define expected benefits; involved in choice	Define logistics objectives and appropriate training; involved in choice
Definition phase	Define type and objectives of partnership	Work out how partners will cooperatively • develop • produce • supply • bill	Mutual knowledge of problems in • quality • production process • packing / shipping
Execution phase	Evaluate partnership, periodic meetings (at least once a year)	Periodic meetings • introduction of new products • modification • continuous improvement	Cooperative order planning and execution

Figure 3-9:   ALP – a model of the formation and operation of partnerships

3.4.4   Quick response (QR)

The first clear movement towards operationalizing the concepts of SCM can be found in the growth of quick response (QR) arising out of the U.S. textile and apparel industry and the Crafted With Pride Council[95] founded in 1984. By the early 1990s, the QR concept had been expanded to embrace integrated partnerships of retailers and suppliers focused on utilization information

---

[94]   SCHÖNSLEBEN/HIEBER, 2000, p. 7.

[95]   LUMMUS, 1997, p. 8.

technologies to speed up quick response to sales demand by distributors and manufactures along the channel pipeline.[96]

In general, QR focuses on shortening the retail order cycle, i.e., the total time elapsed from the point merchandise is recognized as needed, to the time it arrives at the store. The main advantage is to shorten the order cycle and lower the inventory levels required by using new IT, primarily EDI and barcodes to automatically identify products. Hence, QR stems from one single principle – to reduce lead times by conveying sales information from in-store point-of-sales systems to manufacturers via EDI on a same day basis.

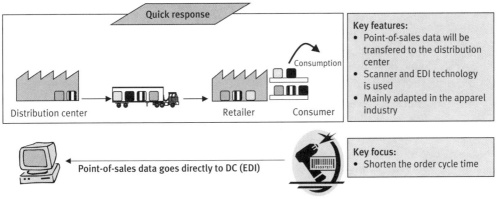

Figure 3-10:   The quick response concept

3.4.5   Efficient consumer response (ECR)

The ECR concept emerged out of the grocery industry in the United States in the late 1980s and early 1990s. The common perception is that ECR is built on QR techniques but it addresses a much wider scope of issues. In 1992, a group of industry leaders created the Efficient Consumer Response (ECR) Working Group[97]. The objective of the group was to investigate the grocery supply chain to identify new technologies and best practices to make the grocery supply pipeline more competitive.

The ECR initiative is designed to replenish inventory on store shelves based on actual consumer demand rather than demand estimation. The ECR's objective is to develop a responsive, consumer-driven approach in which manufacturers, brokers and distributions work together to maximize consumer value and to minimize supply chain costs. To meet this objective, it is necessary to develop a smooth, continual product flow to match consumer consumption as well as

---

[96]   Ross, 1997, p. 97.

[97]   A consulting firm, Kurt Salmon Associates, was engaged by this group to develop a defining document on ECR, released in January 1993. This is generally considered the ECR start date. In Europe, today's members are large consumer product and food companies, including Procter & Gamble, Nestlé, Johnson & Johnsons among others.

provide timely, accurate information flow through a paperless system between the retailer checkout and the manufacturing line. In particular, ECR looks at a product category from a total supply chain perspective, considering packaging and ingredient suppliers, manufacturers, wholesalers, retailers and consumers. Therefore, information must be available to everyone involved in the supply chain.

The ECR concept can be further detailed in three main focus areas and assigned fourteen improvement concepts[98] to help define best practice as follows (see figure 3-11):

- *Category management* – retailers and manufacturers view a group of products as a unit with focus on planning and measuring results, which may include analysis of shopping carts, product range rationalization and store presentation, promotion targeting and capturing electronic point-of-sale data. Key objective is to maximize the effectiveness of the demand creation process.

- *Efficient replenishment* – the purpose of efficient replenishment is to ensure the smoothest possible physical flow of products to the retailers' shelves, which may include consolidation of key raw material and packaging suppliers, cross docking where products from multiple locations are brought into a central facility, re-sorted by delivery destination and shipped within the same day, as well as continuous replenishment (CR).

- *Enabling technologies* – this is a necessary aspect of category management and efficient replenishment by enabling moving large amounts of data concerning supply and demand at the stock keeping unit (SKU) level, which may include EDI systems, electronic funds transfer which electronically exchanges billing and payment information, and item coding and database management (e.g., using barcodes to accurately track products).

---

[98]   www.amteam.org (March 2001).

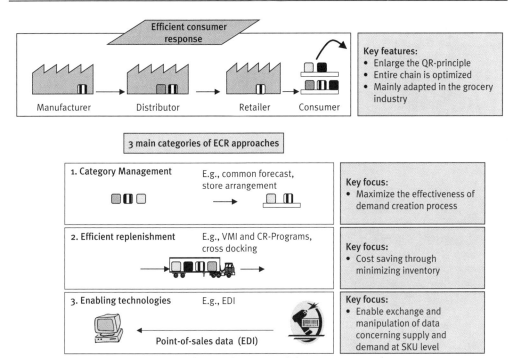

Figure 3-11:   The three basic elements of the ECR approach

3.4.6 Continuous replenishment (CR) and vendor managed inventory (VMI)

Recently, companies from a wide variety of industries have adapted and transformed the underlying principles of the industry-specific ECR as well as the QR concepts into a general demand and supply paradigm, called continuous replenishment (CR). The key idea is to transform from a push logistics down the supply chain towards a pull logistics up the supply chain driven by actual customer demand.[99] Through forwarding the information on actual inventory levels from the customer site to its supplier as a replenishment signal, the suppliers can generate its own delivery schedule to satisfy customer demand (see figure 3-12). Furthermore, specific guidelines and inventory tolerance values must be defined (e.g., safety stock, minimum and maximum levels, etc.) and, at this stage, no planning initiative of the supplier is expected.

An enhancement of this concept towards an even more integrated approach is the vendor managed inventory (VMI) concept. Here, the visibility of the customer's forecast such as promotions and production rates is shared with the suppliers. The planning process using the customer's information is used by the

---

[99] These concepts are widely in place in the leading retailers like Wal-Mart, Whirlpool, Hewlett-Packard and others (see also Ross, 1997, p. 97).

supplier, which now assumes the entire role for planning and replenishment.100 In this case, the supplier takes over the entire planning cycle and fulfills customer demand without a formal delivery schedule from the customer.

Consignment inventory occurs when the supplier physically gives the product to the customer for use and the supplier retains the title of the product until used. The supplier periodically inventories the consigned product and as a result bills the customer and replenishes consigned inventory[101].

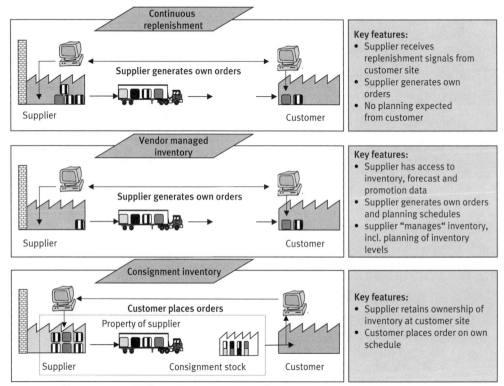

Figure 3-12:   Different transcorporate inventory concepts

3.4.7   Collaborative planning, forecasting and replenishment (CPFR)

The CPFR initiative, founded in 1996 as the Voluntary Interindustry Commerce Standard (VICS) Association[102], has the goal of developing integrated business processes as well as supporting technologies for collaboratively forecasting and

---

[100]   APICS, 2000, p. 27.

[101]   APICS, 2000, p. 8–27.

[102]   Members include Eastman Kodak, JC Penny, KMart, Nabisco, Procter & Gamble, Wal-Mart, etc. For the full list, see the CPFR Web site www.cpfr.org (April 2001).

planning between manufacturers and retailers in order to increase the efficiency of the supply chain.

CPFR operates as a set of business processes and provides guidelines with which trading partners can agree on mutual business objectives and measures, develop joint sales and operational plans, and electronically collaborate to generate and update sales forecasts and replenishment plans. Thus, CPFR collaboration requires information technology to build, share, and adjust on-line forecasts and plans. As figure 3-13 depicts, some implementations of CPFR use a shared database, with interactive trading partner access provided via Web browsers. Other use a peer-to-peer approach, in which servers at each trading partner synchronize their views through message interchange. In more detail, CPFR implementations can encompass eight different types of exchanged messages[103] as follows:

- *Forecast:* Projected demand for an item sourced at a seller location and consumed at a buyer location.

- *Forecast Revision*: A set of proposed changes to a forecast, as the result of promotional activity, weather, distribution or transportation issues, replanning or some other reason.

- *Product Activity:* Actual product movement observed, which may include on-hand quantities, distribution center withdrawals, or POS.

- *Performance History:* A collection of values gathered for key performance metrics in the trading partner relationship, such as forecast error, sales growth, or the number of emergency orders.

- *Exception Notification*: Indication of a variance from trading partner guidelines for changes in a forecast, differences between partner forecasts, or key performance metrics (forecast error, overstock, etc.).

- *Exception Criteria:* Definition of the threshold for variances beyond which an exception message should be triggered.

- *Event:* Description of a promotion, inventory policy change, or other planned event, along with its expected and actual impacts on the supply chain.

- *Item Information Request*: One trading partner's request to the other to send product activity, forecast, or performance data, when the partner does not automatically send data.

Not all message types are required, depending upon the deployment and collaboration scenario. For example, if two CPFR implementations have shared exception criteria, and have local means of triggering an exception, they do not have to exchange exception notifications.

Thus, CPFR enhances the vendor managed inventory concept and continuous replenishment by incorporating joint forecasting, exception alerts and information request messages. The main benefits achieved through the increased

---

[103]   VICS CPFR 2001, p. 4.

level of communication between partners are that when changes in demand, promotions, or policies occur, jointly managed forecasts and plans can be adjusted immediately, minimizing costly after-the-fact corrections for both parties.

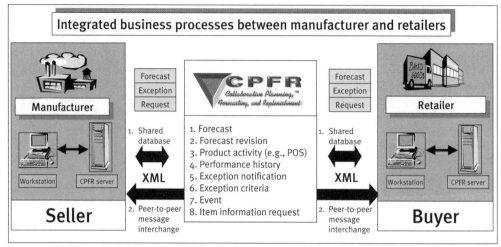

Figure 3-13:   Collaborative planning, forecasting and replenishment concept

A more detailed generic business model with all respective process steps as well as the data flow between the supply chain partners is provided on the public area of CPFR homepage[104].

3.4.8   Third and fourth party logistics

The growth of logistics outsourcing such as transportation and warehousing to external service providers has increased over the last several years. However, while the primary driving forces previously were to reduce costs and release capital for other purposes, the driving forces today are to increase market coverage, improve the level of service or increase flexibility towards the changing requirements of customers. Cooperation between the parties is taking on a more long-term nature and solutions are tailored to specific services, often including value-adding services such as final assembly, packaging and quality control, to name a few. This broader, flexible cooperative arrangement is termed third party logistics[105]. As a consequence, an entire industry – third-party logistics – has emerged to fill the demand for integrated services. Traditional single-service providers remain in place in the form of trucking companies, warehouse operators, and so on, managed and synchronized by third-party companies.

---

[104]   See www.cpfr.org – guidelines and model description (May 2001).
[105]   SKJOETT-LARSEN, 2000, p. 112.

An enhancement of this concept is the so-called fourth party logistics. Nowadays, the execution and operation of the physical transportation and distribution process is not the only focus, but also all the related planning activities[106] of the entire supply chain. In integrated service agreements, the provider offers to take over the whole or large parts of the supply chain, including the management, planning and control of logistics activities, facility management and personnel administration. Those services will be tailored to the requirements of the customer and typically include a number of value-adding services. Partial integration of the parties' information systems will be often necessary, and transcorporate teams of employees from the different entities will emerge.

3.5   IT applications for supporting transcorporate logistics

Information technology (IT) is an important enabler for efficient supply chain management and many IT applications have gained popularity recently, due to their ability to facilitate, coordinate and integrate the flow of information across the supply chain. In the following, the IT innovations in SCM software and electronic data interchange (EDI) applications will be discussed in more detail because of their relevance and wide-spread use as well as the possibilities that are introduced by these technologies in the field of transcorporate logistics, besides bar-coding, scanning technologies, data warehouses, network technology and others. It is interesting to note that several of these IT innovations have been available for a number of years, however, the application to transcorporate logistics is a relatively recent phenomenon[107].

3.5.1   Supply chain management software application

Current SCM software applications support to a very large extent most of the tasks identified in section 3.4.1. The range goes from strategic network design, demand planning, supply network planning to advanced planning and scheduling (APS) applications[108]. In contrast to current ERP systems, SCM applications are not transaction-processing systems in the sense that they record data and process the day-to-day business tasks (e.g., SAP R/3). In general, these are analytical systems that use 'advanced' planning engines (e.g., solver from ILOG with linear, integer or mixed programming as well as heuristics optimization algorithms) that manage the flow of products and information throughout the logistics network of trading partners and customers by analyzing the different constraints (material, capacity, customer requirements, and so on) to create the most feasible plan. Through these algorithms and the ability to capture new

---

[106]   JOHANNSEN, 2001, p. 2.

[107]   HANDFIELD/NICHOLS, 1999, p. 29.

[108]   KNOLMAYER/MERTENS/ZEIER, 2000, pp. 105.

types of information, SCM software applications facilitate the management decision process, which increases flexibility and speed in operations in real-time[109]. In this respect, SCM applications are a new generation of business software. Figure 3-14 demonstrates the use of this new type of business software.

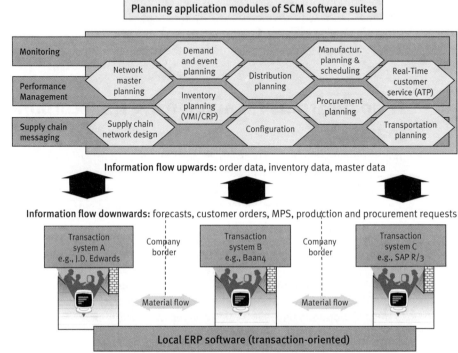

Figure 3-14:   Concept of SCM software application[110]

As figure 3-14 reveals, ERP systems are still the backbone of all the information systems. These systems deliver all the necessary data input for the transcorporate planning and execution parts. For linking together the different ERP systems, and to get all necessary data input into the APS and supply chain network applications, SCM middleware must be in place. This is still the most crucial part of all implemented integrated SCM applications because of the different data structures existing in the ERP systems. So far, SCM applications have mainly been used internally by huge companies or by very powerful customers within a strategic network[111,112].

[109]   KAHL, 1999, p. 61.

[110]   HIEBER, 1999, p. 246.

[111]   SCHÖNSLEBEN/HIEBER, 2000, p. 10.

[112]   AMR, 2000 or Yankee Group, 1998.

3.5.2   Electronic data interchange (EDI) application

Electronic data interchange (EDI) refers to a computer-to-computer exchange of business documents in a standard format (see table 7 below for its relationship to the different industries). EDI encompasses and describes both the practice and the capability of communicating information between two organizations electronically instead of the classical way (letter, fax, phone). Thus, not only the practice of linking together the computer systems of different partners for better communication, but also the capability of an organization to willingly share and effectively utilize the information exchanged is a key component of EDI. It allows members of a supply chain to reduce paperwork and share information on invoices, orders, payments, inquiries, and scheduling among all channel members, hence creating benefits by quick access to information, better customer service, improving tracing and expediting, billing and other activities.[113]

Industry-specific standards	Non-industry specific standards
VDA – Automotive Industry	EDIFACT (ISO7372) – Electronic Data Interchange for Administration, Commerce and Transport) – standard in commerce documents
SEDA – Retailing and Commerce	
SWIFT – Financial Business (banks, insurance)	
GAEB – Construction Industry	ODA/ODIF (Office Document Architecture) – standard in office documents
ETIM/ELDANORM – Electronics Industry	
DATANORM – Distribution and Retailer Business	

Table 7:   EDI standards and formats

In general, EDI improves productivity through faster information transmission as well as reduced information entry redundancy. However, EDI systems are still very expensive and costly to maintain, and thus only large companies with the necessary critical amount of transactions are the main users. Nowadays, a new cost-efficient possibility for SME is offered by Web-EDI. Hereby, the EDI application is not an in-house system, but through a simple Internet access, HTML or Java documents and forms can be processed and posted to an external hosting system, which finally converts the documents and transforms them to the customer's or supplier's EDI system.

---

[113]   HANDFIELD/NICHOLS, 1999, p. 31.

3.6   Summary of existing SCM concepts and techniques

Related to the identified elements of transcorporate logistics in section 3.2.4, the existing concepts and methods are mapped according to content and scope (see figure 3-15).

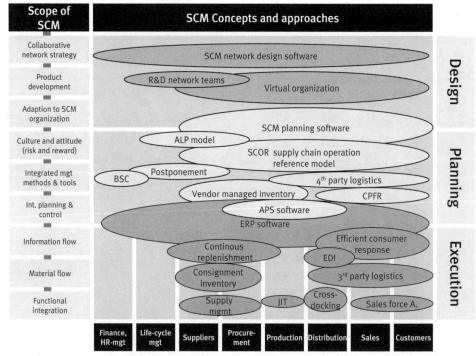

Figure 3-15:   *Various SCM concepts and techniques related to content and scope[114]*

Nowadays, the concepts mainly applied in industry, like VMI or third party logistics, are strongly related to the execution level with the focus of improving the material and information flow. The tendency towards more planning-related elements in transcorporate logistics can be observed more and more often. The current SCM planning software applications play a major role, especially here. The reason why this new approach is located so 'high' in the figure is that when implementing this type of software, collaboration must be a prerequisite and significant changes in organization structures will follow if this type of software is to operate successfully. SCOR is a very promising approach that provides an integrated management method and supports the development of collaboration through mutually designed planning and execution processes along the entire supply chain.

---

[114]   HIEBER/HARTEL/BURKHALTER, 2001, p. 13.

4 Dimensions of characteristic features of industrial logistics networks

In this chapter, the relevant respective characteristic features of industrial networks with regard to transcorporate logistics will be discussed. Using a combination of parameter values of the features in the dimensions of collaboration, coordination, and configuration, specific types of industrial logistics networks can be identified. The focus is on the question of what kind of specific logistics support and services have to be developed for companies operating in this type of network or what are appropriate depending on the respective network type.

4.1 Characteristic features of logistics networks

In the relevant literature (see SCHÄFER 1971, GROSSE-OETRINGHAUS 1974, KUNERTH 1974, SCHOMBURG 1980), a number of different morphological schemes with respect to corporate logistics exist, which make it possible to find suitable reference business process models and planning and control methods for products and product families with certain feature values[115]. Newer approaches and further developments and enhancements can be found in LUCZAK ET AL. 1998, SCHÖNSLEBEN 2000.[116] However, most of these approaches are still focused narrowly on the individual corporate logistics system and only few characteristics can be reasonably applied to transcorporate logistics networks.

---

[115] SCHOMBURG, 1980, p. 34.
[116] Further explanations regarding feature values are given by SCHÖNSLEBEN, 2000, pp. 112–128.

Based on the new requirements for transcorporate logistics, a new integrated approach with appropriate characteristic features for describing the entire industrial logistics network must be developed. In addition to the existing morphological schemes in corporate logistics, the following three new dimensions of characteristic features – *collaboration, coordination and configuration* – applied to a network dimension should be thought of as an enhancement of the existing approaches. The objectives are:

- To offer an easy-to-use methodology for a rough description and characterization of industrial logistics networks.

- To record the key features in transcorporate logistics and to communicate them between the network partners to generate a common language and a transcorporate network understanding.

- To draw conclusions on the mandatory network capabilities to be developed or, respectively, the appropriateness of current transcorporate logistics concepts and methods in place (e.g., planning and control concepts[117], performance measurement approach).

- To offer support with regard to the rough selection of IT systems for logistics networks.

Morphological schemes are most suited to specify and demonstrate the specific characteristics of networks. Morphological schemes are sets of features with each feature having certain possible values that allow analysis and evaluation of all possible stages of a particular situation in the given feature dimension[118]. The evaluation of an object with respect to the given features leads to a pattern, which can be analyzed for finding interrelations between these features. More important for this work, typical patterns can be associated with specific types of industrial logistics networks and give an indication about which transcorporate logistics concepts and methods are most appropriate for this type of network. In this context, this approach should be seen as the starting point when investigating the requirements for new transcorporate logistics concepts in general. In a second step, the existing approaches are still necessary for determining the internal corporate specific morphological scheme.

It is important to know that the following morphological scheme (see tables 8, 9 and 10) should be mutually discussed, completed and agreed with all partners in a logistics network who are willing to start a supply chain initiative jointly, which can finally end up with common performance metrics for the entire network (see chapter 6). This can be the first step to come to a common understanding of the network and to get a deeper knowledge of the interactions between each member. Therefore, cooperation between all participants on all dimensions is the key prerequisite for an efficiently operating logistics network.[119]

---

[117] Using similar methodology, for instance, existing approaches for evaluating PPC software vs. nowadays this new approach for SCM software (see also LUCZAK ET AL., 1998).

[118] ZWICKY, 1989, pp. 14.

[119] SCHÖNSLEBEN, 2000, p. 61.

Furthermore, when applying these morphological schemes, most of the time a logistics network is already in place and in operation and thus, the proposed scheme can be helpful in achieving the above-stated objectives, rather than using them as a tool for selecting appropriate partners for building an entirely new logistics network. However, it can also be a very helpful tool when replacing a partner in the logistics network.

As already stated, the morphological scheme encompass three dimensions – the dimension of collaboration, coordination and configuration – which are closely linked to the model of the advanced logistics partnership model[120] (see section 3.4.3) as well as the SCM task reference model (see section 3.4.1).

- The *dimension of collaboration* describes the degree and kind of partnership between the participants on a high level and the fundamental commitment to a common 'network strategy'.

- In the *dimension of coordination*, the characterization of the daily operations of common transcorporate processes and methods in the logistics network is of main concern.

- The third, the *dimension of configuration*, is the modeling of the existing business relationships between the network entities determined and set up by the two previous dimensions. Here, the physical structure and the timely as well as legal business relationships are described.

The following section discusses each new network dimension of characteristic features and its associated parameter values. As in existing approaches, while the features are independent of each other, individual parameter values can certainly relate to other values.

4.1.1   Features related to describing logistics collaboration

Table 8 shows the first dimension of characteristic features for describing the collaboration in logistics networks.

- *Alignment of network strategy and interests:* On a scale ranging from common network strategy and common network interests to divergence of network interest, this feature describes how focused the common interests to an integrated operating of the network and the consequential overall optimum of the entire network are. Indicators can be agreements on quick time-to-market for new products, quality expectations, target market segments, expected volumes, pricing, desired overall growth rate of network partners, as well as efforts towards technological capability consistent with each partner in the network.

---

[120] In the ALP model, three levels of interaction among suppliers and customers were also identified: the strategic level, technical-commercial level and the operation level.

Collaboration-related features of logistics networks

Feature	➡	Values				
Alignment of network strategy and interests	➡	Common network strategy		Common network interests		Divergence of network interests
Orientation of business relations	➡	Cooperation-oriented		Coopetition/ (opportunistic)-oriented		Competition-oriented
Mutual need in the network	➡	High, sole sourcing	Single sourcing, (A-supply)		Multiple sourcing, (B/C-supply)	Low, highly substitutable
Mutual trust and openness	➡	High				Low
Business culture of network partners	➡	Homo-geneous/ similar		Comparable (e.g., size, structure, volume of sales)		Heteroge-neous/ highly different
Balance of power	➡	High dependency/ hierarchical				Equal/heter-archical

Increase of complexity of collaboration

Table 8:   Values of collaboration features of logistics networks

- *Orientation of business relations:* One key feature of collaboration is related to the type of orientation of the business relations between the network partners. Business relations can be either cooperation-oriented or competition-oriented.[121] In between, the notion opportunistic or coopetition[122] is used, where competition as well as cooperation elements exist. Indicators for a competition-oriented relationship are, for example, if one partner puts pressure on its partners by demanding inflated prices for components[123] or takes advantage of a short supply situation on the world market or, in contrast, re-quoting unilaterally the prices of its suppliers, whereas cooperation-oriented relationships strive for a balancing of costs and rewards.[124] However, the

---

[121] CHRISTOPHER, 1998, p. 246.

[122] Term defined by BOUTELLIER, 2001 as a combination of cooperation and competition elements.

[123] BOUTELLIER, 2001, p. 21: Case study *in the automotive industry:* Example of opportunistic partnership by non-transparent cost structure in a shortness situation on the world market.

[124] LYSONS, 2000, p. 72.

combination of competition and cooperation is regarded as a basic characteristic of most currently observed logistics networks.[125]

- *Mutual need in a network:* Mutual need characterizes the dependency of the network partners among themselves. If the relationships are highly specialized and are only directed towards the existing partners of the network (sole sourcing in the network), there is a high mutual need. For instance, as soon as one business partner would leave or no longer fulfill his agreements in the network, the whole network could no longer act as an entity[126]. In contrast, most of the suppliers of standard components or non-direct goods, are highly substitutable and therefore not as important as the key partners.

- *Mutual trust and openness:* This feature is closely related to the previous one, however, the focus here is on the communication and social structure between network partners. This feature describes the amount of mutual trust and respect in the network. Indications for a high amount of trust and respect can be that all participants keep personal or informal agreements between each other and keep to what they say. In addition, the amount of sharing sensitive information about processes, market analysis and future products gives indications about a trustful relationship. Mutual trust and openness is heavily correlated to the previous two features: orientation of business relations and mutual need. Assuming there is a high degree of cooperation-orientated relationship and mutual need, mutual openness and trust should have been developed simultaneously.

- *Business culture in a network:* Another essential feature for characterizing logistics networks is the perceived business culture between the partners. You can distinguish between a very homogenous social and corporate culture, that means, the employees of the corresponding business units have the same background and education and that most of the time, the companies are all of the same size and organizational structure, whereas an heterogeneous structure can often be found between small and medium-sized enterprises (SME) and global concerns. Therefore, in literature, the notion of incompatibility of corporate philosophies is also used.[127]

- *Balance of power:* The most important factor to be analyzed is the balance of power in the network, for instance, if there is one dominant partner who has significant influence on all the other participating partners.[128] Indicators can be that this partner has a major impact on the information systems to be used (e.g., need for building up EDI connections) or makes frequent significant changes to the delivery schedules on a short notice to its suppliers.[129] This disparity of power exists most of the time because of economic dependency

---

[125] PFOHL, 2000, pp. 388–342.

[126] The most famous case could be observed in the automotive industry where the lack of door closer from a specific company shut down the complete production line of the FORD company.

[127] LYSONS, 2000, p. 71.

[128] SYDOW, 1992, p. 83; BALING, 1997, p.158.

[129] HIEBER, 1998.

based on the difference in size and volume of sales of the participating companies. Especially in this constellation, it is important for the leading company not to seize its power as the ALP model proclaims and demonstrates (compare Section 3.4.3).

4.1.2   Features related to describing logistics coordination

A second morphological scheme is now presented to provide further details on the characterization of the type of coordination in logistics networks (see table 9).

The most synergies with existing approaches can be seen here, especially to the features referring to production and procurement orders.[130] However, a lot of these features can significantly vary between the participating companies in the network and most of the decisions must be defined by the individual company, e.g., the production concept (make-to-stock or make-to-order) and hence, no overall statement for the entire logistics network can be given.

- *Intensity of information sharing:* On a scale from none – limited to the needs of mere order execution, to forecast exchange, order tracking and tracing and sharing of inventory and capacity levels to high – sharing as required for planning and execution of logistics processes, this feature describes how much information is distributed as well as accessible and available for the network partners[131].

- *Linkage of logistics processes* defines the linkage and integration between the partners in a network[132]. The values are closely related to the information sharing practice in the previous feature mentioned above:

  - *Integrated execution* (e.g., continuous replenishment) occurs for instance, through forwarding the information on actual inventory levels from the customer site to its supplier as a replenishment signal. The suppliers can generate its own delivery schedule to satisfy customer demand.

  - *Vendor Managed Inventory* (VMI): VMI differs from consignment models in several aspects. The visibility of the customer's forecast such as promotions and production rates is shared with the suppliers. The planning process using the customer's information is used by the supplier, which now assumes the entire role for replenishment *and* planning [133].

---

[130] SCHÖNSLEBEN, 2000, p. 123.

[131] Compare also information models in SCHMID, 1998, p. 143.

[132] Compare also logistics reference model in ZILLIG, 1998.

[133] APICS, 2000, p. 8–28.

Coordination-related features of logistics networks					
Feature	➤	**Values**			
Intensity of information sharing	➤	Limited to needs of order execution	Forecast exchange	Order tracking and tracing	Sharing of inventory/ capacity levels	As required for planning and execution processes
Linkage of logistics processes	➤	None, mere order execution	Integrated execution (e.g., conti-nuous re-plenish-ment)	Vendor managed Inventory	Collabo-rative planning	Integrated planning and execution
Autonomy of planning decisions	➤	Heterarchical, local indep. autonomous decisions		Local decisions with central coordination guidelines		Hierarchical, led by strategic center
Variability of consumption (execution)	➤	Low/stable consumption	Variability in time	Variability in amount		High variability in time and amount
Extent of formalization (long-term orders)	➤	None, regular purchase orders	Blanket order: capacity			Blanket order: goods
Degree of com-munication between multiple tiers and channels	➤	Single contact for the transaction	Regular network meetings (e.g., sup-plier days)	Central coordination (e.g., supply chain manager)		Multiple contacts between levels and channels
Use of information technology (IT)	➤	IT use only for supporting internal business processes		IT use to support network coordination mechanisms (e.g., EDI)		IT use to support execution and planning mechanisms (e.g., SCM-SW)

Increase of complexity of coordination[134]

---

[134] Complexity of coordination (e.g., amount of effort) from the logistics network point of view, not from an individual partner

Table 9:   *Values of coordination features of logistics networks*

- *Collaborative planning decisions:* A first step towards collaborative planning decisions can be collaborative forecasting (see section 3.4.7), which implies an agreement between trading partners to jointly develop a single shared forecast plan, which can become the foundation for all internal planning activities related to that product or product family. Changes outside of the parameters require approval of the partners involved. This approach should help trading partners generate the most accurate forecast possible[135]. In further steps in linkage, the logistics planning processes, and not only forecast plans, are generated in the above-mentioned way, but also further planning activities (e.g., master and delivery schedules) are adapted to the overall needs of all participating partners.

- *Integrated Planning and Execution:* Here, all planning and execution activities are managed and coordinated by a central function. Most of the time, this can be observed in global concerns, which operate a central logistics unit, which is responsible for the leverage of demand and supply of the 'self-owned' network, mainly supported by a SCM software application[136]. Furthermore, only a few cases already exist where this approach is extended over the company's own organizational boundaries.

- The amount of influence of a particular partner in a network during the logistics planning is described according to the feature of *autonomy of planning decisions.* Possible values of this features are:

  - *Local autonomous decision:* In this case, each network partner comes up with its own procurement, production, distribution and forecast plans and no communication between the planners occur.

  - *Central planning decisions* exist when one key leader in the network prepares the planning numbers for the entire network. This can be the case for example in the automotive industry, where the OEM has a significant influence on the supply network as well as in corporate groups where one central position determines the plans and schedules down to the shop floors for all affiliated divisions.

  - *Local decisions with central guidelines* exist in the case where the plans and schedules are not completely defined, but general guidelines for all partners are available.

- *Variability of consumption* has a significant influence on the degree of necessary coordination in the network. The range can vary from very few variations, which lead to stable schedules up to a high variability of consumption in time and amounts over time. The less variation identified in the network, the simpler the IT system for coordination of the logistics

---

[135]   www.cpfr.org – Guidelines and business reference models for demand planning processes (May 2001).

[136]   E.g., central logistics planning of Hoffmann-LaRoche – in conference proceedings, IBM/ETH Zurich, 1. SCM Software Forum, 1999.

network can be (e.g., simple spreadsheet solution). In this context, these variations can also be due to the described Bullwhip Effect (see chapter 2) and can be documented in this manner.

- *Extent of formalization:* A high amount of formalization implies clearly defined rules and procedures in preset basic logistics contract agreements. This can be operationalized by blanket orders. A blanket order is a type of purchase order that is issued to a supplier that indicates an estimated usage of the item for a predetermined period of time at a negotiated price[137]. Most of the time, this is the case in stable and long-term relationships and, as a consequence, can minimize the problem of small orders that are used repetitively. This type of contract can also be applied on capacity[138] assigned to a product family. The partners can then refer to formal agreements as well as standard procedures in the network. In contrast, no logistics agreements can exist, which lead to the standard procedure of coordination of a regular purchase order.

- *Degree of communication* between multi-tiers and channels describes the interaction and formal contacts between the participating network partners[139]. The range can vary from just contacts with the previous and subsequent persons, regular network meetings, contacts organized by supply chain manager/network coordinator, to multiple contacts between the involved levels and logistics channels. An example for the value 'regular network meetings' are the so-called 'supplier days' in the automotive industry where the OEM invites important suppliers, regardless of industry branches, to communicate new long-term strategies (e.g., products, long-range forecast, market development and so on).

- The scope of network information technology can be described by *use of information technology*. This feature reveals the extent of IT use in the area of transcorporate logistics. The values differ from the mere internal use (e.g., own ERP-system), some network coordination IT tools (e.g., EDI), to IT usage to support execution and planning coordination activities (e.g., SCM software).

4.1.3   Features related to describing the configuration of logistics networks

The third morphological scheme is presented to further describe the characterization of the configuration of logistics networks (see table 10). Cooperation consists of at least of two partners and, based on the definition of cooperation, are linked by a dyadic[140] relationship to each other. However, as

---

[137]   APICS, 2000, p. 8–45.

[138]   SCHÖNSLEBEN, 2000, p. 125.

[139]   WILDEMANN, 1996, p. 214.

[140]   Twofold, made up of two units.

soon as three and more organizations are working cooperatively with at least some shared objectives, the term network organization will be used.

Configuration-related features of logistics networks					
Feature ➡	**Values**				
Multi-tier network (depth of network) ➡	2 value-adding tiers		3–5 value-adding tiers		>5 value-adding tiers
Multi-channel network (breadth of network) ➡	1–2 logistics channel(s)		3–5 logistics channels		>5 logistics channels
Linkage between the partners ➡	Simple relationship, segmentation				Complex relationship, ramifications
Geographical spread of network ➡	Local	Regional		National	Global
Time horizon of business relationship ➡	Long-term, >3 years		Mid-term, 1–3 years		Short-term, less than 1 year
Economic and legal business involvement (financial autonomy) ➡	Group / combine		Alliances		Independent business partners
Increase of complexity in logistics configuration					

Table 10:   Values of configuration features of logistics networks

- *Multi-tier network (vertical integration):* This feature takes into account the number of tiers of the network formed by the participating value-adding units. By definition, at least, two tiers are necessary to form a simple relationship. These can be either internal units within the boundaries of a global concern or external units encompassing several independent business partners. For instance, in the following case study (see figure 4-1), three value-adding tiers within a globally active company have been taken into account in the network analysis.

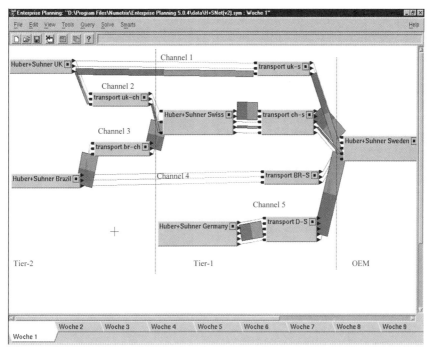

Figure 4-1:   Mapping of logistics network configuration in SCM software[141]

- *Multi-channel network (horizontal integration):* A logistics channel refers to the stream of information, materials, components, and assemblies that are associated with a particular final product or product family. This definition is quite similar to the definitions of supply chains, however, the focus lies on the flow of goods and less on the different participating companies or plants, which often lead to confusion. Based on this definition, several logistics channels can be operated between two companies, whereas, based on the classical definition, only one supply chain can be identified. Nowadays, trends towards logistics service provider concepts can be observed where these providers try to operate the entire logistics channels (see also section 3.4.8).

In SCHOMBURG (1980), a similar approach for describing and characterizing the product structure can be found. There, the depth of product structure and breadth of product structure is defined as the key features related to the appropriateness of PPC concepts and methods to be used. In ALBERTI (1996), this approach has been further developed for the concept of the complexity number of product structure[142]. Similar to this, the underlying concept can be translated to the physical structure of networks because the new resulting requirements on the transcorporate logistics management is not only described by the product

---

[141]   HIEBER, 2000, p. 267.

[142]   In this approach, a two column product matrix is build whereby the first column contains the vector T based on the number of components of each level, and the second column contains the vector B based on the number of subassemblies of each level. By weighting the number of parts of each level with the corresponding level, the complexity number K can be build, which is a indicator of the complexity of the product.

structure itself, limited by the company's boundaries, but also by the different linkages between partners who are participating in the entire value-adding processing chain.

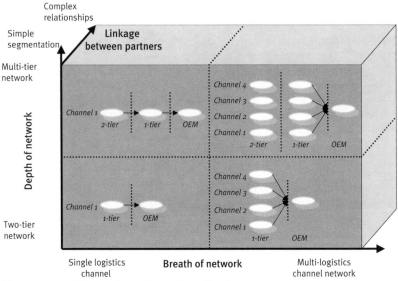

Figure 4-2:   Physical configuration of networks

The number of logistics channels and tiers describes the basic structure of the physical network. By adding a third dimension, the degree of linkage of business relationships between the partners, the entire complexity of the physical logistics structure of the network can be described.

- *Linkage between the partners:* Here, the values can range between simple point-to-point relationships (segmentation) up to complex relationships, that means, one partner in the analyzed logistics network not only delivers the subsequent tier, but also over a different logistics channel, to additional partners on different tiers[143]. This generates several options, especially in global distribution networks, which contributes to a tremendous complexity. An example of an analyzed network, modeled in SCM software, with a three tier and five logistics channel structure, which still has a very simple segmented relationship structure – mainly 1:1 relationships and only few ramifications, is demonstrated in figure 4-1.

- *Geographical spread of network* distinguishes between local, regional, national and a global dimension and thus, covers all possible methods of geographical spread. Nowadays, numerous cooperations emerge on a local or regional geographical basis, when important suppliers settle near the enterprise to be supplied. This development is mainly apparent in the automotive industry. On the other end, on a global dimension, large

---

[143]   BOUTELLIER, 2001, p. 18.

enterprises form strategic alliances to be present in all regions and markets of the world and therefore build up mostly legal dependent subsidiaries in the target market.

- *Length of time of business relationship* is determined by the strategic objectives of the cooperation of the partners in the network. Smaller projects, for instance, R&D activities, can be realized on a short-term time horizon, whereas economies of scale by an integrated production network most of the time emerge in long-term business relationships. However, e-business is contributing significant changes in this field and allows new types of cooperation over time and hence new network models (compare section 4.2.2).

- *Economic and legal business involvement (financial autonomy):* Enterprises are characterized by acting independently, decisions are based on their own initiatives and none or only a few extent external decision instructions exist[144]. Thereby, the notion of autonomy encompasses the legal and economic independence. Whereas, the legal independence is easily proven by the legal form of a company, the operationalization of the economical independence is much more complex to determine. Economic independence exists when a company can make a strategic decision and transfer it on their own. Furthermore, a small financial involvement of the partners can contribute to a certain stability of the network by demonstrating the common intention to cooperate[145].

Using these three morphological schemes, a general overview of the current state of the logistics network can be observed and the first insights of the appropriateness of transcorporate methods and concepts can be gained. Based on these three dimensions of characteristic features, specific type of logistics networks can be identified, which are described in the next section.

4.2   Specific types of industrial logistics networks

Based on the three morphological schemes, it is possible to structure the observed variety of several relevant characteristic features in networks and offer a useful simplification of reality and, as is the purpose of this approach, provide an opportunity to describe logistics network in its entirety.

Using these features, the following section identifies and describes three relevant types of industrial logistics networks. Related to figures 4-4, 4-5, and 4-6, there are three main network types called strategic networks, supply chain networks, and e-communities. This typology draws on the work of SYDOW (1992), SCHOLZ (1994), MERTENS (1995) and PFOHL (2000). Using the two key network features 'time of business relations' and 'balance of power', a network portfolio

---

[144]   SYDOW, 1992b, p. 78.
[145]   MÜLLER-STEWENS/HILLIG, 1992, p. 68.

can be drawn (see figure 4-3). However, strict transition stages cannot be identified, thus overlapping areas can occur between different network types. At first sight, strategic networks are characterized by a high complexity of configuration and a low level of complexity of cooperation, while e-communities are described by the opposite side. In general, supply chain networks, the latest identified network type, is described by a high level of logistics structure as well as collaboration complexity. In general, all three network types have a high degree of coordination complexity in common.

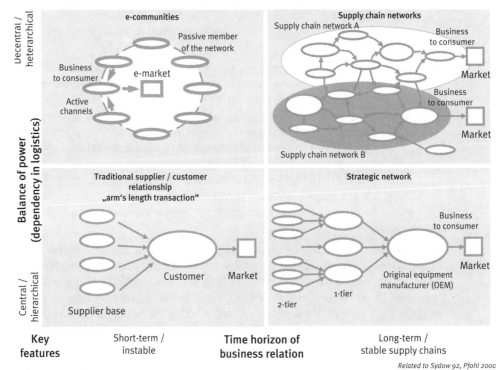

Figure 4-3:   Types of logistics networks[146]

In the following, the most distinguished features and some examples will be explained.

4.2.1   Strategic network

Strategic networks, the most often cited network type in literature (SYDOW, 1992, JARILLO, 1993), is guided strategically by a large core enterprise, which is often a retailer or manufacturer close to the final customer. The network is relatively stable and oriented towards the joint achievement of strategic advantages. The member enterprises are usually closely linked to the core enterprise but also

---

[146]   HIEBER/ALARD, 2001, pp. 202–209.

offer their product to customers outside the network to preserve a bit of their autonomy and competitiveness. This network form is well suited to serve a comparatively stable market[147]. Well-known examples are networks in the automotive industry[148] and industries where the core enterprise 'owns' several tiers as well as operating its own logistics channels. In this case, the central logistics unit can be responsible for coordinating several business units along the supply chain and can even determine the plans and schedule down to the shop floor.

Therefore, another key feature is the use of information technology. These enterprises are still the main users of current available SCM software applications[149], which mainly support these kinds of central coordination. The structure of the network can be very complex, and the amount of coordination is enormous. However, it should be mentioned that in this type of network, a very intensive sharing of information is quite easily possible because of standardized, industry-specific IT interfaces (e.g., VDA standards), which allow easy access to the information system. The complexity of collaboration is finally quite low because of the homogenous business cultures, common network strategy and most of the time, the long and stable business relations (e.g., 'internal' supply chains in a global concern).

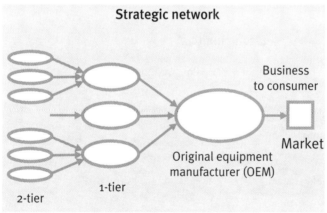

Figure 4-4:   Strategic network

4.2.2   E-communities

A new type of network are e-communities (see figure 4-5). By the universal adoption of the Internet, a unique opportunity for companies arose to develop new business models by using this kind of new information technology. From almost anywhere, companies can quickly, at short notice, get access to other

[147]   PFOHL, 2000, pp. 391.

[148]   MÄNNEL, 1996.

[149]   AMR, 2000.

business partners' information systems and can execute the necessary transactions with the business partner over the common web platform. In this respect, the network shows some similarities to virtual enterprises, but is generally larger in the number of participating partners, shorter in business relations, and heavily dependent on information technology and hence, the transcorporate information system forms the basis for the common network.

Therefore, the intensive use of information and communication technologies as well as the absence of a hierarchical 'control' and dependence between the members are the key characteristics of this type. The transactions are relatively standardized and concern single value-adding activities rather than complex processes[150]. Most of the time, this type of network reveals a simple logistics structure, mainly only tier-to-tier relationships of the supply chain, and are close to the final market. However, the cooperation is quite complex based on the divergence of network interests, the highly substitutable business partners, and heterogeneous culture of the business partners, which finally leads to a high degree of collaboration complexity.

The best examples for this type of network are the current business-to-business (B2B) exchange networks or B2B marketplaces. Numerous web-based exchange platforms connect buyers and suppliers in real-time and add value by allowing buyers to leverage their purchasing power to gain influence.

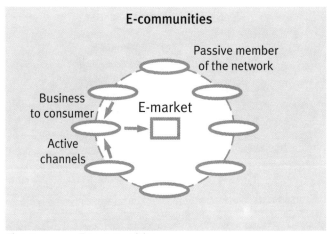

Figure 4-5:   E-communities

Furthermore, most of the B2B activities in e-communities falls under the category for non-direct goods. Therefore, existing e-communities simply bring together a huge number of buyers and sellers with a fixed price menu, and hence help cut transactions costs (e.g., covisint.com, eSteel.com, healtheon.com and others). In contrast to these big open e-marketplaces, opportunities for SME can also be identified[151] for this type of network. By forming short-term networks defined and

---

[150]   PFOHL 2000, p. 394.

[151]   REINHART, 2001, p. 39.

configured by the necessary specific competencies of each partner, enabled and supported by Internet technology, for the requested demand of the marketplace, new ways of collaboration can be identified. Examples are: www.RP-Net.de in the area of rapid prototyping, www.produktionsnetz.de in the area of manufacturing, and www.engineering.de in the area of R&D.

4.2.3   Supply chain network

Supply chain networks are a fairly new type of identified network. They consist of independent enterprises that are working together to exploit a particular business opportunity by offering a product jointly to the market, based on common interests and partnership-oriented business relations (see figure 4-6). Here, the objective is to coordinate logistics activities across the entire network to create value for the final customers, while increasing the profitability of every member in the network. Furthermore, there is no predominating partner in the network, which leads to a balance of power. Still, there can be differences in size and sales volume, however, none of the network partners takes advantage of its position.

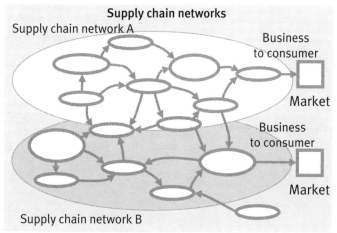

Figure 4-6:   Supply chain network

This type of network requires a high degree of mutual trust, respect and openness. To operate efficiently, the network and the necessary logistics information must be shared. This leads to a very high degree of coordination complexity. However, though not as easily as in strategic networks, this can be realized. Here, the specialty is that network partners in this type of network can be integrated in several different networks, so there is serious resistance to sharing sensitive logistics information, especially on-hand inventory or available logistics and production capacities[152]. As the Swiss survey revealed in section

---

[152]   As the survey results in the Swiss industry in section 2.3.6 revealed, this type of network is still in the development stage.

2.2.3, the general perception of managers is that sharing rich information with suppliers would give them too much power in the relationship, and therefore, as the results show, many supply chain relationships witness limited information exchange. Moreover, information technology in supply chain networks could contribute to efficiently coordinating the logistics activities, however, current SCM software packages do not fulfill the specified requirements[153]. Even more issues occur when trying to apply current performance measurement systems, which heavily rely on financial data, to the entire network.

As the above described network types represent ideal types, there will, in reality, be many transitional forms exhibiting features associated with two or more different forms. Nevertheless, these ideal types will be useful as a frame of reference for the following performance measurement approach that will focus on 'supply chain networks' as the center of interest.

In summary, most of the companies, especially small and medium-sized companies, are currently operating in supply chain networks, but still cannot fully operationalize the concepts of SCM – as the Swiss survey revealed. To support this type of network, a performance measurement approach will be proposed to speed up this transition.

---

[153]   See project results CTI ProNet No. 4209 and 4674.1.

5

5 Approaches and key requirements for performance measurement

One component of supply chain management that had been relatively neglected until recently was the domain of supply chain performance measurement[154]. In the following chapter, new requirements for a collaborative performance measurement as a result of the developments in transcorporate logistics will be derived, existing approaches briefly presented and finally, an evaluation of the existing approaches of performance measurement concerning their appropriateness for industrial logistics networks discussed.

5.1 The seven principles of performance measurement in logistics networks

In recent years, a number of companies realized the potential of supply chain management. However, they often lacked the insight necessary for the development of the effective performance indicators and metrics needed to achieve a fully integrated supply chain[155]. Furthermore, such indicators were required to test the viability of SCM strategies and without such strategies a clear direction for improvement and the realization of objectives could not be implemented by the network partners.

---

[154] HANDFIELD/NICHOLS, 1999, p. 61.

[155] GUNASEKARAN/PATEL/TIRTIROGLU, 2001, p. 72.

The characterization of logistics networks represents a suitable starting point for the analysis of the respective requirements of a transcorporate logistics performance measurement (see section 4.1). Hence, an appropriate performance management tool must align itself with the specific, characteristic features with respect to the network dimensions of logistics collaboration, coordination and configuration and therefore, the performance measurement approach must be methodically as well as institutionally differentiated based on the respective network type.

In the following section, the requirements for a new collaborative performance measurement system for logistics network will be derived. The main focus of these considerations is the identified supply chain networks, which are the most complex and challenging type of network to be supported, caused by the high degree of complexity in collaboration and configuration (compare section 4.2.3).

5.1.1   Integrated supply chain approach – network-oriented

Network partners pursue different objectives when participating in a logistics network. Some partners can strive for shorter lead times, others for significant know-how increase and further partners for developing new markets. As soon as several organizations with different corporate objectives and interests, different corporate cultures and different policies are included, the new challenge is to integrate them in a collaborative way towards a common logistics network objective.

Therefore, the new performance measurement approach must support an integrated view on a global as well as a local performance perspective and hence must not be inconsistent with the corporate performance measurement approaches which are in place. As a matter of fact, with the new approach, an entire end-to-end view of the considered logistics network must be enclosed and supported. That means, all relevant tiers and channels of the network should be included to prevent network entities from acting as autonomous units instead of components of the entire logistics network, and thus neglecting the width and scope of their interdependencies with other network entities. As a result, a superior top-level performance measurement approach should be provided which supports a common collaborative perspective on the logistics network. Furthermore, the contribution as well as the interaction with the local performance approaches must be consistent to diminish the potential conflicts of interests.

5.1.2   Collaborative approach – partnership-oriented

From a collaboration point of view, the partnership orientation in logistics networks is the most important. The results of numerous studies investigating critical success indicators in SCM, have shown (e.g., TOWILL 1997, NEW 1996, FRIGO-MOSCA/ALBERTI 1995, HIEBER ET AL. 2000) put stress on the prerequisite of a win-win partnership for an efficient and successful supply chain management.

Accordingly, the extent of the partnership that exists between the entities in the logistics network must be evaluated and improved as well. Several 'partnership-evaluation' criteria have therefore already been developed (e.g., level and degree of information sharing and the scope and stage at which the supplier is involved by TONI ET AL. 1994, the extent of mutual assistance in problem solving efforts by MALONI AND BENTON 1997 and others), but are not included or only considered to a very small extent in existing performance measurements.

This dimension must be highlighted in particular and included in a performance measurement approach for logistics networks, which will lead to a more collaborative logistics network perspective.

5.1.3   Financial vs. non-financial approach – balanced-oriented

Many companies have realized the importance of financial as well as non-financial performance measures, but mostly failed to understand them in a balanced framework. According to KAPLAN AND NORTON (1992), while some managers and researchers have concentrated on financial performance measures, others have concentrated on operational measures. Such an inequality does not lead to metrics that can present a clear and integrated picture of organizational performance.

As suggested by MASKELL[156] AND JOHNSON[157], for a balanced approach, companies should bear in mind that, while financial and accounting-based information plays an important role in strategic planning and for monitoring financial results, it is less suitable for controlling and improving activities.

In addition, success in business today is not solely determined by a strong cash flow. Instead, developing competency, capabilities and skills in areas such as supply chain-based problem solving, IT innovation (e.g., setting up information exchange channels) and new logistics concepts are much more important, yet not easily measured in financial terms. Hence, a new performance measurement approach should overcome the existing issues and should lead to a more balanced approach.

5.1.4   Integral logistics approach – business process-oriented

The supply chain management concept has its fundamental origin in a business process-oriented approach. However, while most of the existing performance indicators are still allocated to functional entities from a top-down perspective (e.g., costs of acquisition of material by aggregation over several functional levels to report to the chief financial officer), a more logistics business process-oriented approach will lead to a better understanding and evaluation of the

---

[156]   MASKELL, 1991.

[157]   JOHNSON, 1990, p. 64.

entire process of serving the final customer in a logistics perspective[158]. Thereby, the problem emerges that 'controller figures' are based on financial accounting or reporting systems and are not easily compared with 'engineering and logistics figures' focused on the movement of goods and pieces in volumes and flows[159]. For example, it is not obvious how, in a functional point of view, inventory carrying costs or material acquisition costs contribute to the overall performance of the entire supply chain, instead of, in a more process-oriented view, the amount of inventory on-hand of a product, stocked in a logistics channel from the supplier up to the final customer.

5.1.5   Hierarchical approach – multi-level-oriented

The logistics objectives associated with performance measurement in SCM clearly varies between different levels in and across organizations. Based upon the different tasks to be fulfilled in a strategic, tactical or operational context, appropriate performance indicators must be provided. Furthermore, in order to guarantee the complete integration and the transition between the different levels, the chosen performance indicators must be build upon each other hierarchically. Ideally, each performance indicator should be assigned to a level where it would be most appropriate and should lead to its superior and inferior measures. Thus, by demonstrating the interdependencies between the different levels, the cause and effect relationships in supply chain management can be analyzed in more detail[160]. However, this is one of the most challenging requirements because not only the increase in complexity by the number of respective participating partners in the network, but also the several levels of the organizations must be taken into account. Thus, to handle the described complexity, the recommended top-down approach of BSC or SCOR can be a promising solution to overcome these issues. Most advanced in this field is SCOR, which encompasses such a performance hierarchy[161] (see Appendix C).

5.1.6   Systematic approach – model-oriented

On the strength of a systematic approach (e.g., EFQM-model, Malcom Baldrige Award), the performance measurement for logistics networks should be supported by a generic framework to give guidelines on how to implement and use the recommended performance measures. This model should provide a self-assessment 'tool-box' to ease the start of a collaborative performance measurement and structure the required steps in a systematic manner. The amount of effort for recording and operating the collaborative performance

---

[158]   MERTENS, 1999, p. 389.

[159]   HOLMBERG, 2000, p. 856.

[160]   However, as table 12 reveals, most existing corporate approaches fail to come across any such hierarchical approach.

[161]   WIENDAHL ET AL., 1998, p. 22.

measurement approach must be kept low, which can best be supported by using a model-based approach.

In general, a systematic approach should support a simple, structured and meaningful performance evaluation while providing a limited powerful number of performance indicators in order to reveal the current degree of logistics objectives achievement in a comprehensive way.

5.1.7   Adaptive and scaleable approach – scope-oriented

With respect to the level of detail, the network performance measurement system should contain any desired eligible elements, thus each 'network' can tailor its specific scope and objectives after deriving them from overall set network targets and strategies. At the same time, it should be scaleable to any desired size of network. However, quite often companies already have a large number of performance indicators to which they keep adding indicators in order to monitor new problem areas, and they fail to realize that performance measurement can be better addressed using a few good metrics[162]. Consequently, the network indicators should be limited in order to counteract the consumption of more and more resources, while adding little value. As a consequence, network partners should concentrate on a few, clear, meaningful indicators for logistics.

Furthermore, as most strategic tasks in SCM are dealing with future events, the indicators should not only be based on historical data, but also potential developments and trends must be taken into account by an appropriate performance measurement, which will finally lead to an adaptive approach.

5.1.8   Final remarks and conclusions

Most of the above-described principles for a performance measurement approach are already more or less quite familiar and accepted on a corporate level, however, not from a network perspective as yet. Thus, most of the above principles are nowadays included in recently developed performance measurement approaches as table 13 will reveal and, as the result of the previous discussion has shown, it seems reasonable to include them in a logistics network context. However, regardless of the performance approach selected on a corporate level, the primary focus must be on supporting a logistics network perspective. Therefore, striving for the lowest common achievable denominator on network objectives and assigned performance metrics approved in a collaborative manner of each participating partner (see figure 5-1) should be an objective.

---

[162] GUNASEKARAN ET AL., 2001, p. 72.

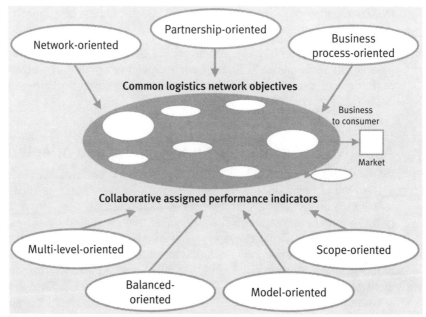

Figure 5-1   Requirements for a collaborative performance measurement approach

In conclusion, based on our research on the efficient management of a logistics network, the performance measurement must fulfill and support a network-, partnership-, balanced-, business process-, multi-level-, model- and scope-orientation, which contributes to an overall logistics network perspective.

5.2   Current approaches for measuring performance in industrial practice

Research scientists and business organizations have shown an increasing interest in improving the design of measurement systems during the last few years. Several reports (e.g., Harvard Business School Council on Competitiveness Project[163]) have expressed concern with the current overemphasis on financial measurements of business performance and revealed the limitation of such approaches. As a result, the Balanced Scorecard (BSC) approach of KAPLAN AND NORTON has awakened particular interest and has been widely disseminated. These two authors stated that the overemphasis on achieving and maintaining short-term financial results can cause companies to overinterest in short-term fixes and to underinvest in long-term value creation, particularly in the intangible and intellectual assets that generate future growth[164].

---

[163]   www.compete.org (August 2001).
[164]   KAPLAN/NORTON, 1992, pp. 71–79.

Historically, the origin of today's most popular performance measurement can be traced back to the early 1950's. Called *the Du Pont performance measurement chart system*[165], it leads to the single key performance indicator: *'return on investment'* (ROI). The Du Pont chart system propagates that a manufacturing enterprise can best measure and judge the effectiveness of its efforts in terms of the single metric 'return on investment', which is the product of two percentages – earnings as per cent of sales multiplied by turnover. Therefore, the charts utilized and submitted to the executive management every third month, are designed to place primary emphasis upon this ratio[166].

In the following, the most popular approaches will be briefly discussed to demonstrate the main differences between the various approaches.

5.2.1   The Balanced Scorecard approach

The Balanced Scorecard by KAPLAN AND NORTON is probably the best known measurement framework at present.[167] The two authors claim that the Balanced Scorecard approach translates an organization's mission and strategy into a comprehensive set of performance indicators that provide the framework for a strategic measurement and management system. By offering a multidimensional scorecard, the balance between financial and non-financial should be provided. They argued that in today's business, financial indicators provide poor guidelines, because the financial model measures events of the past, not the investment in the capabilities that provide value for the future[168]. Moreover, the Balanced Scorecard retains an emphasis on achieving financial objectives, but also includes the performance drivers of these financial objectives[169].

The scorecard measures organizational performance across four balanced perspectives (see figure 5-2):

- *Financial perspective*
- *Customers perspective*
- *Internal business processes perspective*
- *Learning and growth perspective*

---

[165] The Du Pont chart system was first presented outside the company's home office at an AMA Financial Management Conference in December 1949 under the leadership of T.C. Davis, the treasurer of Du Pont.

[166] AMA, 1960, p. 5.

[167] As a result of a study which was motivated by a belief that existing performance measurement approaches, primarily relying on financial accounting measures, were becoming obsolete, conducted by the Nolan Norton Institute, research arm of KPMG in 1990.

[168] KAPLAN/NORTON, 1996, p. 18.

[169] KAPLAN/NORTON, 1996, p. 2.

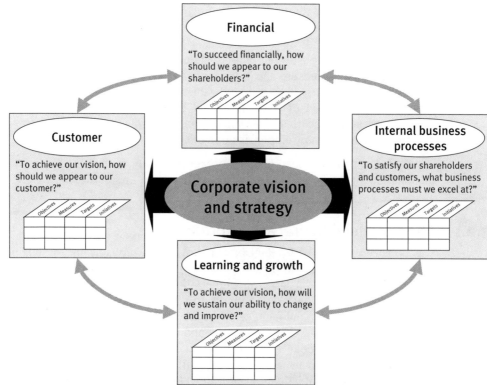

Figure 5-2:   Balanced scorecard approach (Kaplan/Norton)[170]

In the financial perspective, performance indicators show whether a company's strategy, implementation, and execution are contributing to bottom-line improvement (e.g., operating income, return-on-capital-employees). In the customer perspective, managers identify customer and market segments in which the business unit will compete and the measurement of the business unit's performances (e.g., customer satisfaction, customer retention). In the internal business process perspective, the organization identifies the critical internal processes in which the organization must excel and finally, the fourth perspective, learning and growth, identifies the infrastructure that the organization must build to create long-term growth and improvement. Figure 5-3 shows the generic indicators of the BSC approach, which show up in most organization's scorecards[171]. However, when implementing Balanced Scorecards, company specific indicators must be still derived from the organization's own strategy.

---

[170]   KAPLAN/NORTON, 1996, p. 76.

[171]   KAPLAN/NORTON, 1996, p. 44.

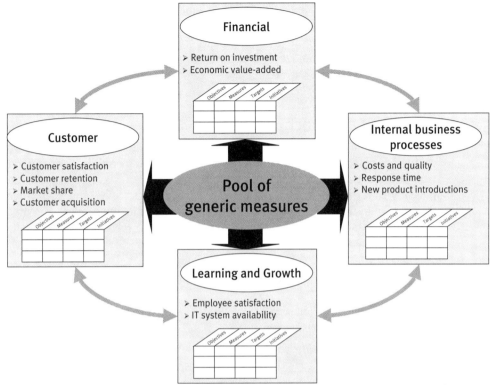

Figure 5-3:   Example of generic performance indicators of BSC-approach

Furthermore, the scorecard tries to minimize information overload and information shortage by focusing on a handful of indicators that are most critical for describing the performance of the company. With 12–15 performance metrics, the critical indicators of the enterprise should be balanced[172].

In addition, the BSC should be used to articulate the strategy of business, to communicate the strategy as well as to help align individual and organizational initiatives to achieve a common goal. Used in this way, the scorecard does not strive to keep business units in compliance with a pre-established plan, as traditional control system objectives. The BSC should be used as a communication, informing, and learning system, not a controlling system[173].

In relation to supply chain management, APICS propagates the extension of a BSC approach towards logistics networks and demonstrates its potential use for logistics networks by introducing BSC for different levels (supply chain, organization, function, team/individual scorecard)[174].

---

[172]   WEBER/SCHÄFER, 2000, p. 1.

[173]   KAPLAN/NORTON, 1996, p. 25.

[174]   APICS, 2000, p. 9–46 and Handfield/Nichols, 1999, p. 64.

In conclusion, the Balanced Scorecard retains financial measurements as a critical summary of managerial and business performance, but it highlights a more general and integrated set of measurements that link current customers, internal processes, employees, and system performance to long-term financial success[175].

5.2.2   The SCOR approach

One way to improve the transcorporate collaboration between the network partners is to share a common framework of terminology and business practice (see section 3.4.2). Therefore, the Supply Chain Council developed a standard glossary of terms, management processes and metrics, called the SCOR model (Supply Chain Operations Reference Model). As one of its major parts, the model encompasses several key performance attributes and metrics that permit it to analyze and evaluate supply chains against each other.

On the top level of SCOR, five categories, called the 'SCOR Performance Attributes' for supply chain metrics, are defined:

- *Supply chain delivery reliability*
- *Supply chain responsiveness*
- *Supply chain flexibility*
- *Supply chain costs*
- *Supply chain asset management efficiency*

Associated with these performance attributes are the key performance indicators, the so-called level 1 metrics (see table 11). Corresponding to the Supply Chain Council, these level 1 metrics are the calculations by which an implementing organization can measure how successful they are in achieving their desired positioning within the competitive marketplace.

Metrics in the SCOR model are intended to decompose from or lead to these five attribute categories, that means, all further detailed and more company-specific metrics can be categorized in these five sections and are sub-metrics of these 13 top metrics. Thus, the performance measurement approach of SCOR is strictly hierarchical. However, the direct relationships, for instance, the aggregation from a level 3 metric to the level 1 metric and vice versa is not given yet[176].

---

[175]   Kaplan/Norton, 1996, p. 21.

[176]   According to an interview with chief technology officer Scott Stephens at the SCOR Workshop in Hanover, November 28th–29th, 2000, these hierarchical relationships will be included in the next version 5.0.

Supply chain delivery reliability[177]	Supply chain responsive-ness	Supply chain flexibility	Supply chain costs	Supply chain asset management efficiency
Delivery performance Fill rates Perfect order fulfillment	Order fulfillment lead times[178]	Supply chain response time[179] Production flexibility	Cost of goods sold Total supply chain management costs Value-added productivity Warranty/returns processing costs	Cash-to-cash cycle time Inventory days of supply Asset turns

Table 11:   SCOR level 1 performance metrics (version 4.0)[180]

The metrics and performance attributes will be discussed in more detail in chapter 6, given that the model will serve as the basis for an integral performance measurement for supply chain networks.

5.2.3   ENAPS process performance model

ENAPS stands for the European Network for Advanced Performance Studies project, which was funded by the European Union within the ESPRIT 20888 project[181]. The objective of the project was to establish and test a permanent European network for advanced business process performance studies in European industry. The main results from the ENAPS project were a methodology consisting of a generic business process framework and corresponding performance indicators (see figure 5-4). The developed performance indicators that support the generic framework are structured around the business level, the process level and the main activity or function level with the measurement dimensions time, cost, quality, volume, flexibility and environment. In addition, the manufacturing typology is used to ensure that relevant indicators are developed for different manufacturing environments. To describe and monitor the performance indicators, a measurement cube is used to offer tangible classification of business processes as well as measurement dimensions (BRADLEY AND JORDAN, 1996).

---

[177]   In former version of SCOR Models denoted as "Delivery performance/Quality".

[178]   Times associated with cycle time measurements – full definition in Appendix C.

[179]   Predictive measurement associated with unplanned demand movements – full definition in Appendix C.

[180]   For definitions, see Appendix C.

[181]   www.cordis.lu for further details (April 2001).

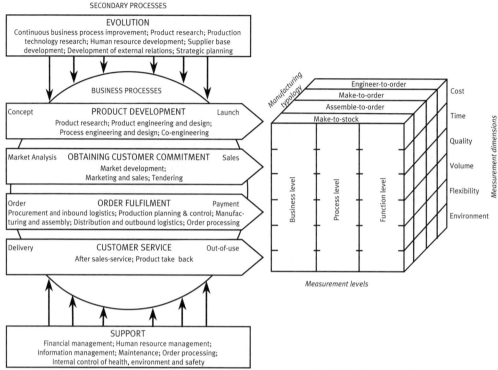

Figure 5-4:   Generic model of the ENAPS approach

However, while the model and concept are very well described and documented in literature, there are only few examples of the applied framework and the related performance metrics.

5.2.4   Standards in logistics performance measurement

The VDI guideline[182] 2520 'practice-oriented characteristic values for logistics in small and medium-sized companies' provides some suggestions for the development of a corporate performance measurement system. The objective of such a system should be to allow the permanent monitoring and control of the overall logistics system at the company's interfaces relevant to performance and costs as well as to provide metrics, which are practice-oriented and relevant to decision making[183]. The main focus is on the logistics activities of storage, movement and distribution. By taking into account the general corporate structures, nine basic performance metrics were selected, which were derived from targets, that should be common to the target hierarchies of almost every company (see figure 5-5). Furthermore, detailed description, encompassing

---

[182]   VDI – The Association of Engineers is a financially independent and politically unaffiliated, non-profit organization of 130,000 engineers and natural scientists (www.vdi.de August 2001).

[183]   VDI, 1999, p. 3.

calculation formula, sources of the data necessary for calculation, and differentiation possibilities were provided.

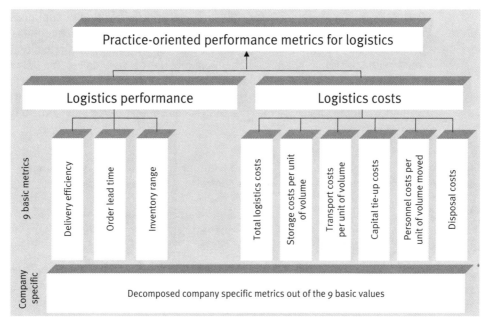

Figure 5-5:   Basic performance indicators of VDI guideline 2520

In addition, the VDI guideline states that such performance metrics must be individually tailored to meet the requirements of each company as the priorities among the logistics activities, depending on the type of company and the industry branch, may vary greatly. Thus, the nine key logistics metrics presented should serve as a basis for the development of an individually balanced performance measurement system. Depending on the needs of the company, the metrics can be broken down in more detail and supplemented as applicable. Requirements on such performance metrics are up-to-date, clearly arranged, meaningful, generally comprehensible, and manageable in terms of amount. Finally, these performance metrics should be revised periodically. Furthermore, the VDI guidelines recommend that after gaining initial experience with the performance metrics, to fine-tune the company-specific performance measurement system with a view to achieving a comprehensive corporate logistics system[184].

---

[184]   VDI 1999, p. 8.

5.2.5   SCM software application and performance measurement

Performance measurement for logistics networks is already supported by modern SCM software applications in which predefined performance measures, also called key performance indicators (KPI), can be found. In this context, the most popular supply chain management module of SAP, called the Advanced Planner and Optimizer (APO), should be mentioned. Here, performance indicators are stored in a business data warehouse and can be accessed from SAP APO/Supply Chain Cockpit, the central control unit of APO, by launching 'KPI queries'.

Quality/ service	Production control	Supply chain flexibility	Inventory control	Supplier performance	Human resources
Delivery performance	Schedule/ lead time deviation	Cycle times	Stock values/ quantities	Supplier on-time delivery performance	Average headcount
Returns		Pro-duction lead time			
Deliveries	Order quantity		Inventory turnover	Supplier fulfillment rate	Employees' average age
Fulfillment rates		Supplier cycle time			
Incoming orders	Detailed order release deviations		Finished goods/raw material in-ventory	Delivery schedule variance	Productivity rate
Credit memos					
Sales values			Days of sup-ply quantity/ value		
Order, delivery and sales quantities	Scheduled achievement		Inventory obsolete	Delivery quantity variance	Overtime rate

Table 12:   Dimensions and metrics for performance measurement in SAP APO

These performance indicators express abstract supply chain objectives in financial or physical units for comparative purposes[185]. Data pertaining to the various planning processes such as demand planning or production planning is collected, measured and transformed into physical or financial information that can be used to compare results and thus measure performance. SAP APO KPIs include some SCOR metrics and some that have been developed by SAP. For example, one of the supply chain flexibility metrics is Supplier On-time Delivery Performance, which indicates the percentage of orders that are fulfilled on or before the original requested date. Table 12 shows a list of some of the defined

---

[185]   SAP Library release APO 1.1.

KPIs. These APO KPIs cover a wide variety of business areas: quality/service, human resources, production, purchasing, inventory control, finance, and controlling.

5.2.6   Performance measurements from related research fields: the EFQM-model

Performance measurement has a wide range of research areas and many ongoing research efforts covering various aspects. One very important research area in performance measurement has been in the field of total quality management (TQM). From the beginning of the last decade, the subject of TQM has been studied and practiced, and has been reported extensively in the literature. As a consequence, several TQM models have been developed, whereby the Deming Prize, the Malcom Baldrige National Quality Award (MBNQA) and the European Quality Award (EQA) have been well established in industry and furthermore, are the most recognized. Because of its importance for the European area, the most popular model, the EFQM-model[186] will be discussed shortly in order to show the generic framework and scope rather than the detailed specific performance metrics.

The European Foundation for Quality Management's (EFQM) mission is to stimulate and assist organizations throughout Europe to participate in improvement activities leading ultimately to excellence in customer satisfaction, employee satisfaction, impact on society and business results; and to support the managers of European organizations in accelerating the process of making total quality management a decisive factor for achieving global competitive advantage[187].

Therefore, the following model, a non-prescriptive framework based on nine criteria, has been introduced and applied successfully in several industries since 1996[188]. Five of these criteria are 'Enablers' and four are 'Results'.

- The *'Enabler' criteria* cover what an organization does.

- The *'Results' criteria* cover what an organization achieves. 'Results' are caused by 'Enablers'.

The EFQM-model is presented in diagrammatic form below (see figure 5-6).

---

[186]   The European Foundation for Quality Management (EFQM) was founded in 1988 by the presidents of 14 major European companies, with the endorsement of the European Commission. The present membership is in excess of 600 organizations ranging from major multinationals and important national companies to research institutes in prominent European universities.

[187]   See www.efqm.org for further information (April 2001).

[188]   The EFQM-model is the basis for the European Quality Award, a process which allows Europe to recognize its most successful organizations and promote them as role models of excellence.

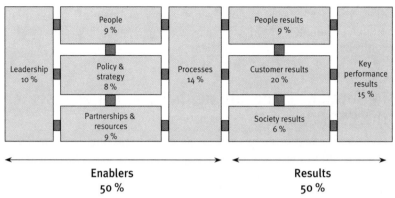

Figure 5-6:   EFQM excellence model

The model is especially intended to serve as a framework for organizations to help them develop their vision and goals for the future in a tangible, measurable way, and have its most significant impact as a diagnostic tool for assessing the current health of the organization, also known as self-assessment. Self-assessment is a comprehensive, systematic and regular review of an organization's activities and results referenced against the EFQM Excellence Model that allows the organization to discern clearly its strengths and areas in which improvements can be made and culminates in planned improvement actions, which are then monitored for progress.

After identifying the new requirements for performance measurement in a logistics network context and indicating the most often applied and relevant approaches in performance measurement, the appropriateness of these approaches will finally be evaluated for logistics networks.

5.3   Comparison of existing performance measurement approaches

In the following, a comparison and evaluation of the appropriateness of the existing performance measurement approaches will be shown when applied to logistics networks. The main differences of the underlying approaches as well as their strengths and weaknesses should be revealed and demonstrated.

This will help identify the best qualified elements for a new performance measurement for logistics networks as well as to find out the most promising approach, which will then serve as the baseline for the proposed approach. Based on those findings, specific recommendations for enhancement and adoption can be initiated.

Key requirements on performance measurement for logistics networks	SCOR	Balanced Scorecards	VDI Standard	SCM Software	EFQM-Model	ENAPS framework
Network-oriented – Supporting all relevant partners – Integrated vs. non-integrated elements – Focusing on an end-to-end view ('big' picture)	◉	○	○	◎	◎	○
Partnership-oriented – Include explicitly collaborative elements – Adaptability to the extent of partnership – Stresses win-win situation	○	◎	○	○	◉	○
Balanced-oriented – Financial vs. non-financial elements – Past vs. future oriented – Internal vs. external view	●	●	⊙	⊙	●	◉
Business process-oriented – Integral logistics orientation – Supporting logistics planning and execution processes – Providing 'logistics' figures	●	⊙	◉	◎	⊙	●
Multi-level-oriented – Supporting hierarchical structure – Strategic, tactical and operational elements – top-down methodology – Cause-and-effect relationships	◉	●	⊙	●	○	⊙
Model-oriented – Including specific guidelines (e.g., self assessment, implementation) – Including definitions and instructions	●	◎	◎	◉[189]	●	◉
Scope-oriented – Adjust to the needs of logistics network objectives – Limited to specific number of generic performance indicators	●	●	◉	⊙	◎	◉

● entirely supported	◉ to a very large extent	◎ partly supported	⊙ to a very small extent	○ none identified

Table 13:   Comparison of different approaches and evaluation of appropriateness

---

[189] Cause of automatic generation through the software itself.

In summary, table 13 reveals that the least met requirements of logistics network performance measurement in the current approaches are collaboration as well as network orientation. Only the EFQM-model partly addresses this area of cooperation in any detailed manner. As a matter of fact, the SCOR model is the most advanced, both in the area of network orientation as well as in the other additional identified areas and therefore will serve as the baseline for the proposed approach.

To overcome the identified shortfalls in the areas of collaboration and network-orientation, an enhancement of the existing SCOR model and an adaptation to the needs of logistics networks will be proposed in the next chapter.

6

6 An integral model of performance measurement

As shown in chapter 5, the prevalent performance measurement approaches have primarily a single focus on internal and short-term operational results in companies. As a consequence, these approaches for performance measurement are not designed to strive for and contribute to the global optimum of industrial logistics network. Thus, new ways and instruments must be developed to contribute more to an integrated and collaborative network perspective approach. In this chapter, a new model will be introduced, which should overcome these deficiencies and provide a framework for measuring performance in logistics networks to meet the identified requirements on performance measurement (see section 5.1). Finally, using SCOR as a basis, a model with the respective performance target areas and assigned performance indicators will be discussed and described in detail[190].

6.1 The objectives of transcorporate logistics

Corporate logistics has a significant influence on enterprise objectives in the areas of quality, costs, delivery, and flexibility. As a matter of fact, most of the current logistics performance measurement approaches are focusing on these four performance target areas. However, transcorporate logistics enlarge the

---

[190] To guarantee the adoption and compliance with SCOR, in the following proposed model the term supply chain will be used as a synonym for logistics network.

perspective from a single company's point of view towards a network system's orientation.

According to our research, the following three new high-level enabling logistics network performance target areas can be identified and are defined as follows:

- *Supply chain collaboration:* The ability to work together and act collaboratively in a win-win partnership to fulfill (final) customer demand in a logistics network. All activities should be oriented towards the global optimum of the logistics network.

- *Supply chain coordination:* The ability of logistics network partners to coordinate and communicate efficiently in daily operations. That means that organizations, people, and systems all have access to relevant logistics information regardless of organization, location or company.

- *Supply chain transformability:* The ability to achieve a high substantial potential of flexibility in (re)configuration of supply chains between the partners in the network by means of practicing and sharing logistics know-how, capabilities, routines, and skills as well as leveraging ideas and visions.

Table 14 reveals the fundamental objectives within the high-level logistics network performance target areas.

Performance target area	Enabling-oriented objectives on network level *(Enablers)*	Result-oriented objectives on network level *(Results)*
Supply chain collaboration efficiency	– to achieve high degree of strategic alignment in the supply chain – to achieve highly integrated business processes, either for planning or execution aspects	– reduced friction losses (global vs. local optimum) – reduced supply chain lead times – reduced transaction costs
Supply chain coordination efficiency	– to achieve seamless information and material flow between the supply chain partners – to achieve high degree of information transparency	– reduced total inventory – higher efficiency of resource utilization – higher inventory turns – higher delivery reliability – speed up logistics decision making
Supply chain transform-ability	– to achieve high potential of flexibility in (re)configuration of supply chains for customer responsiveness	– quicker time-to-market – higher customer responsiveness – maximize value delivered to final customer (consumer)

Table 14:   High-level performance target areas in logistics networks

These network performance target areas are dedicated to the overall optimum of a logistics network and in addition, finally contribute to a very large extent to improvements in transcorporate as well as corporate logistics with respect to quality, costs, delivery, and flexibility.

- *Target area supply chain collaboration:* Within supply chain collaboration, the main objectives are to achieve strategic alignment as well as integrated and collaborative business processes, for planning as well as execution aspects. By achieving this, the local optimization within companies' boundaries should be shifted towards a network systems' perspective in which efforts and attention are directed towards the global optimum of the logistics network. This will contribute to reduced friction losses, reduced supply chain lead times, and reduced transaction costs.

- *Target area supply chain coordination:* The main objective within this area is to achieve a seamless information and material flow along the entire supply chain through efficient information availability needed for logistics planning decisions as well as execution activities. This will finally lead to reduced total inventory levels, higher efficiency of resource utilization, higher inventory turns, higher delivery reliability, and a speed up of logistics decision making on a network level.

- *Target area supply chain transformability:* The main objective listed above is certainly the most valuable, but also the most difficult to achieve as well as to measure. By gaining a high supply chain potential of flexibility in (re)configuration between the partners in a logistics network[191], the better the entire network is prepared for future changes in customer demand and new market requirements and can quickly act upon those. Result-oriented objectives and expected benefits can be quicker time-to-market, higher customer responsiveness, and, finally, maximized value delivered to the final customer.

Thus, these new identified performance target areas of logistics networks enlarge the current perspective towards a more integral view and hence, will be best reported and measured by common transcorporate performance indicators.

To enable this performance measurement for logistics networks, the following integral model with the respective assigned performance indicators will be now proposed.

6.2   An integral model for performance measurement in logistics networks

While most of the current approaches described in chapter 5 provide guidance for the internal corporate performance measurement, the following proposed performance measurement framework will direct attention towards logistics

---

[191]   WESTKÄMPER, 1999, pp. 131–134.

network orientation, by which several entities of a network will collaboratively develop performance indicators to evaluate the performance of the logistics network in its entirety.

Figure 6-1 demonstrates the fundamental concept of the integral model for transcorporate performance measurement.

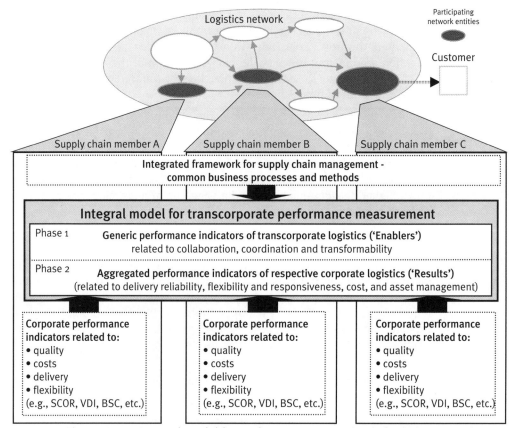

Figure 6-1:   Integral model for performance measuring in logistics networks

The integral model is based on the common practices and processes in supply chain management of the participating network entities who are willing to start a joint performance measurement approach.

Therefore, the integral model consists of generic as well as aggregated performance indicators of the participating companies in order to (self)assess the performance of the entire logistics network. However, as figure 6-1 proposes, a two-phase approach will be recommended.

In phase one, generic high-level transcorporate logistics performance indicators are of main concern *(Enablers)*. These are metrics that mainly address the collaboration, coordination, and transformability performance target areas of the network and record how well the logistics network is operating and less so the results, which are caused by the enablers. As a result of phase 1, the so-called logistics network SCORcard (see figure 6-5) will summarize these high-level generic performance indicators, as discussed and evaluated by the top management of the involved network entities. Especially at this early stage of implementing a common performance measurement system, it is very sensitive to already capture and exchange metrics related to cost information or cost structures[192]. As studies have revealed[193], supply chain partners may be reluctant to share information on costs, internal lead times, or inventory turnovers and in addition, the need to release sensitive and confidential information may compound this hesitation[194]. Hence, at the beginning, the performance indicators will first operate on a high-level logistics network perspective, rather than on the prevalent result-oriented financial and operational perspective.

In phase two, by building trust and openness and setting up efficient lines of communication during the common operations in the network, including monitoring of the generic performance indicators, the integral model can be then enlarged step-by-step with elements of current performance measurement approaches with the respective corporate logistics performance target areas of quality, costs, delivery and flexibility by aggregating and transforming those on a network level (Results (e.g., SCOR, Balanced Scorecards)).

Thus, in phase two it will be possible to combine current corporate performance indicators in place to aggregated 'network' performance indicators. In addition, those will then also incorporate result-oriented performance indicators (e.g., costs) in order to evaluate the overall performance of the entire logistics network in a more operational and financial perspective. Therefore, the most suitable approach for this purpose is the hierarchical SCOR model, as chapter 5 has shown, with the respective performance target areas of delivery reliability, responsiveness, flexibility, costs and asset management efficiency and its assigned metrics, which are then directed towards a logistics network orientation.

In summary, the newly proposed, two-phase integral model encompasses enabling and result-oriented performance indicators to provide the network entities involved with input that identifies areas for improvements within a network perspective and allows them to direct management attention to those network entities that have a high potential for improvement.

---

[192] This is still a very sensitive and debated issue, where many companies want their partners to reveal cost structures, but not give away their own. As a consequence, to overcome these hurdles, this two-phase approach will be recommended.

[193] Compare survey results in section 2.3.6.

[194] HANDFIELD ET AL., 2000, p. 46.

6.2.1   Generic performance indicators in logistics networks

To meet these new requirements and to overcome the existing identified short-falls in logistics network performance measurement, table 15 introduces a new set of high-level generic performance indicators on the transcorporate level[195]. The complete definitions of the metrics is provided in SCOR notation with possible soft as well as hard influence factors assigned to each metric in Appendix B, table 19–21.

Performance target area	Definition	Generic transcorporate performance indicator[196]
Supply chain collaboration efficiency	The ability to work together and act collaboratively in a win-win partnership to fulfill (final) customer demand in a logistics network. All activities should be oriented towards the global optimum of the logistics network.	– Supply chain strategic alignment – Supply chain planning collaboration – Supply chain execution collaboration
Supply chain coordination efficiency	The ability of logistics network partners to coordinate and communicate efficiently in daily operations. That means that organizations, people, and systems all have access to relevant logistics information regardless of organization, location or company.	– Supply chain information availability – Supply chain communication – Supply chain IT-support
Supply chain transform-ability flexibility	The ability to achieve a high substantial potential of flexibility in (re)configuration of supply chains between the partners in the network by means of practicing and sharing logistics know-how, capabilities, routines, and skills as well as leveraging ideas and visions.	– Supply chain know-how – Supply chain skill sharing – Supply chain (re)configuration flexibility

Table 15:   Generic performance indicators (transcorporate level) – 'Enablers'

It is also important to mention, that these performance target areas and assigned performance indicators are the most difficult to record in a quantitative manner. As a consequence, the main interest is not the total score, but more the difference to previous benchmarks. In addition, this proposed set of generic performance indicators should be considered as a starting point for a collaborative performance measurement, rather than a fixed set of predefined indicators. New ones can be added and existing ones can be abandoned, depending on the specific needs of a logistics network.

---

[195]   This table also includes the already stated definitions in order to adapt to the well-known notation of SCOR (compare table 16).

[196]   Defined in SCOR notation in Appendix B, table 19-21, including soft and hard influence factors.

Thus, this set of generic performance indicators is limited to a powerful number of indicators to guarantee the applicability as well as to present the current logistics state in a comprehensive way[197] (compare figure 6-5). These enabling indicators especially can be a useful instrument to discern clearly the strengths and areas in which improvements can be made.

Moreover, by taking into account the critical success factors of logistics networks (see sections 2.2 and 2.3), these nine generic performance indicators should be common to the general logistics transcorporate performance target areas of almost every logistics network. Furthermore, these performance indicators can be further broken down in one of the specific performance target areas as applied in the case studies in chapter 7 in order to fine-tune the specific logistics network needs[198].

In general, this set of performance indicators gives a clear picture of what a logistics network does *(network enabler)* by evaluating the 'quality of cooperation', which will lead towards a more result-oriented financial and operational picture of what a logistics network achieves *(network results)*. It is important to mention that these performance indicators are not inconsistent with the local indicators already in place, they even supplement each other in a integral point of view by adding the new dimension of 'quality of cooperation'.

6.2.2   Aggregated performance indicators in logistics networks

In the second phase of the two-phase approach, the integral model can be enlarged through an aggregation as well as a transformation of current performance indicators towards a transcorporate network level. The most advanced tool for this purpose is the SCOR model and therefore, it will be integrated in this model. Thus, related to this approach, it is possible to aggregate and use these SCOR metrics not only on a corporate level, but also transform them on a transcorporate level for the entire respective logistics network.

The current SCOR model addresses the following performance target areas with assigned performance indicators within the 'plan supply chain P1' process category, which can be considered the 'result' of the generic key performance indicators. The SCOR level 1 performance target areas are:

- *Supply chain delivery reliability*
- *Supply chain responsiveness*
- *Supply chain flexibility*
- *Supply chain costs*
- *Supply chain asset management efficiency*

---

[197] Compare with 5.2.1, which argues that 12 to 15 KPIs are the maximum amount.

[198] Compare also chapter 8 – Outlook in which additional research is recommended to deepen the understanding of the interrelations between these KPIs (IMS-EU project PRODCHAIN).

Table 16 shows the performance indicators assigned to each target area identified by SCOR. The detailed definition of those performance indicators, called SCOR level 1 metrics, is provided in Appendix C, table 22-23.

Performance target area of SCOR	Definition	Corporate performance indicator (SCOR Level 1 Metrics)
Supply chain delivery reliability	The performance of the supply chain in delivering: the correct product, to the correct place, at the correct time, in the correct condition and packaging, in the correct quantity, with the correct documentation, to the correct customer.	– Delivery Performance – Fill Rates – Perfect Order Fulfillment
Supply chain responsive-ness	The speed at which a supply chain provides products to the customer.	– Order Fulfillment Lead Times
Supply chain flexibility	The agility of a supply chain in responding to marketplace changes to gain or maintain competitive advantage.	– Supply Chain Response Time – Production Flexibility
Supply chain costs	The costs associated with operating the supply chain.	– Cost of Goods Sold – Total Supply Chain Management Costs – Value-Added Productivity – Warranty/Returns Processing Costs
Supply chain asset management efficiency	The effectiveness of an organization in managing assets to support demand satisfaction. This includes the management of all assets: fixed and working capital.	– Cash-to-Cash Cycle Time – Inventory Days of Supply – Asset Turns

Table 16:   Performance indicators of SCOR level 1 – 'Results'

It is important to note that, like the process elements themselves in SCOR, the assigned metrics are intended to be hierarchical. Although not explicitly mentioned in this new model or in the current SCOR model version 4.0, these metrics enable the aggregation towards network metrics on a network level as well as a decomposition on subsequent SCOR levels into more operational diagnostic metrics for the respective SCOR planning, execution and enable process elements of the participating network entities.

However, this further aggregation and transformation on a network system's perspective is only appropriate and feasible if the previously mentioned prerequisites of a high degree of mutual trust and openness within an intensive and close-relationship are met. Still, the first step of an network performance measurement system will be the generic performance indicators and, the second step provides the opportunity for the participating network partners to make these enhancements as proposed.

In conclusion, most of these key performance indicators can be already found in current performance measurement approaches (see chapter 5) and can be tracked down to the traditional logistics performance target areas of time, costs, quality and flexibility[199]. However, the innovative idea of SCOR and this new model is the ability to aggregate and decompose the performance indicators to the needs of the various levels within a logistics network.

Thus, by combining the generic and aggregated performance metrics, a powerful set of performance indicators is provided for an integral performance measurement approach for logistics networks.

6.2.3   Integral model as an enhancement of the SCOR model

As already mentioned, the most advanced tool in the area of supply chain performance measurement is the SCOR model, which meets the identified logistics requirements on a network perspective to a large extent (see section 5.3). Hence, the SCOR model will serve as the basis, and most of its notation and structure will be adopted in order to ease the understanding for the SCOR user community as well as to guarantee a possible adoption in subsequent SCOR versions.

As the discussion in chapter 5 has shown, the focus of the SCOR model is mainly on the corporate organization and the internal supply chain[200]. By a combination of the three basic elements: source, make, and deliver and the upper-related planning elements, the 'internal' supply chain is well defined. In addition, this model can certainly be expanded to the next suppliers, as well as to customers, by adding the corresponding source, make and deliver elements. However, as concerns the current plan process elements and assigned performance indicators at level 1 already in place, this implies some major issues and hurdles during implementation. The degree of partnership and cooperation between the partners, as well as the performance measurement of the entire logistics network on a high level dimension, is not taken into consideration. Especially at the beginning of a commonly operated performance measurement approach, the more result-oriented performance metrics of the SCOR model are not suitable for measuring the network performance in a collaborative way (see table 13). The main reason is that independent business partners working together in logistics

---

[199]   SCHÖNSLEBEN, 2000, p. 94.

[200]   SCC Plan Technical Committee, 2001, section 7.1.1 and 7.1.2.

networks are not willing to share that much confidential information, like total order management costs, return on assets, or cash-to-cash cycle times, as the SCOR model proposes[201] when starting to implement and put such a system into practice[202]. Therefore, a new approach to measuring the performance of logistics networks in its entirety is provided by this integral model.

One possible way to demonstrate the underlying idea of a network- and partnership-oriented performance measurement approach, is shown in figure 6-2, which represents the proposed integral model in figure 6-1 as an enhancement of the current SCOR model. Here, a new top-level process category with the newly assigned performance target areas will be introduced, called *Po plan supply chain: transcorporate*, which is shown as a graphical representation in SCOR notation in figure 6-2 as well as in more detail in the following section.

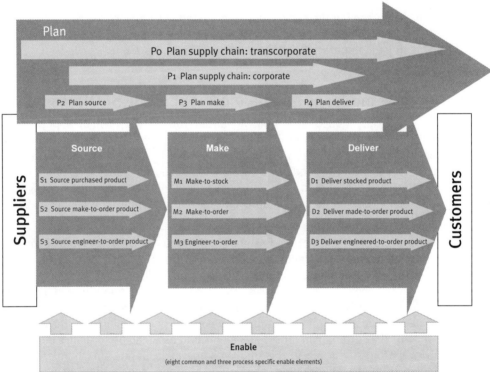

Figure 6-2:   Integral model for performance measurement in SCOR notation

In addition, as figures 6-1 and 6-2 reveal, every partner still has to manage and operate its internal logistics corporate performance indicators, recommended within the existing process *P1 – plan supply chain* consisting of the 13

---

[201]   Except for strategic networks (section 4.3), where the predominate partner can force the participants to disclose these data.

[202]   This can even lead to barriers against implementing the SCOR model, as experiences in the research project ProNet as well as other research have proven (see section 1.2).

recommended key performance indicators of SCOR. As a matter of fact, the overall explicit definitions in SCOR and the resulting common 'language' with the same bases of measurement offers the opportunity to aggregate those SCOR metrics towards 'network' metrics of the new proposed SCOR level 0. To make the difference between these two levels more clear, the extension 'corporate' to the current notation will be recommended, which finally leads then to *P1 plan supply chain: corporate*.

In the following, the proposed new process category *P0 Plan supply chain: transcorporate* will be discussed in more detail.

6.3   Process elements of PLAN supply chain: transcorporate

To give some guidelines and lead the way towards a collaborative performance measurement, the proposed integral model is supported by the following process elements.

In general, this top level PLAN process category (P0) encompasses activities to initialize and configure, analyze, improve and monitor a logistics network with the means of the proposed high-level performance indicators and hence, enables the participating companies to design and manage the logistics network collaboratively in its entirety, which finally leads to common established courses of action for performance measurements and improvements.

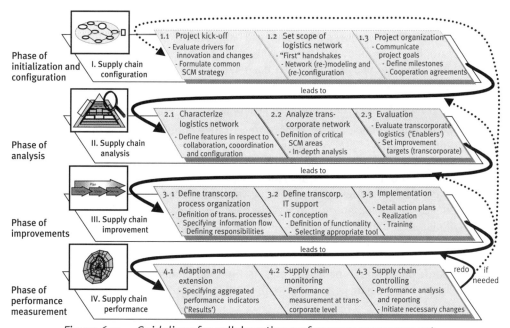

Figure 6-3:   Guidelines for collaborative performance measurement

Figure 6-3 outlines this framework and summarizes the process steps on how to proceed and implement such a collaborative performance measurement. Therefore, the definition of the phases are oriented towards the classical cycle of problem solving, which can be applied to find solutions for complex, less structured assignments[203] (see HABERFELLNER ET AL., 1994).

In addition, to complete the proposed enhancement of the SCOR model, the SCOR notation will be used as the descriptive language for the process elements of *Po Plan supply chain: transcorporate* (see figure 6-4). The detailed description of SCOR notation and definitions can be found in Appendix D, table 24.

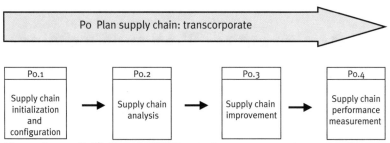

Figure 6-4:   Guidelines in SCOR notation – process elements of Po

It is important to know that these top level processes can only be started and run successfully if top management has committed themselves and several players in the supply chain. Such an initiative needs a supply chain promoter who is able to set up all the personal links to the right people. Still, supply chains are operated by human beings and most of the success is also related to organizational collaboration and communication.

Finally, those process elements will support the implementation of common supply chain initiatives, which will finally lead to the proposed transcorporate performance measurement. The assigned process elements with the respective phases will be now roughly discussed:

- *Phase of initialization and configuration:*

In this first phase, a high level representative should evaluate the need for and introduce the SCM performance measurement and improvement initiative, including a rough limitation of the first scope of the supply chain venture. This phase should result in fundamental agreements that will be upheld by the partners in the logistics network, which establishes the degree of commitment needed for a long-term partnership based on a common defined SCM strategy. Related to these first principle agreements, the general project organization and project assignments can be derived. Additionally, a rough model (useful already in SCOR notation) of the current logistics network with all its respective participants must be provided. As the ALP model postulates, cooperation between all partners is the key condition for a successful logistics network, thus

---

[203]   Which finally resulted in the project management methodology called Systems Engineering.

it is important to involve all participants early on. Only in this way will the consensus and team spirit develop within a network that is essential to transcorporate logistics[204].

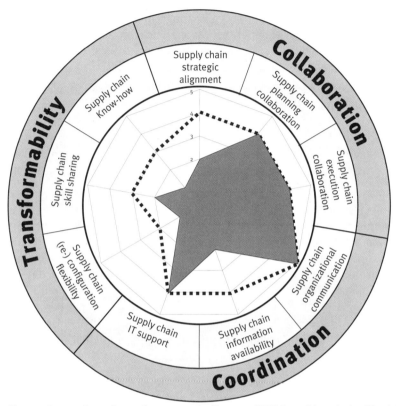

Figure 6-5:   Generic performance indicators 'SCORcard level 0' – 'Enablers'

• *Phase of analysis:*

Analyzing the supply chain is the focus of the next phase. There are several promising analysis techniques discussed in the literature, including a first step of the mapping of information and material flow within the network (e.g., HINES, P., RICH, N. – The Seven Value Stream Mapping Tools[205] or WREDE V.[206]) to detect areas of improvements in supply chain management[207]. In addition, to guarantee an integral view of the logistics network as well as to provide a common language for communication among supply chain partners, the characteristic features for logistics network (see chapter 4), mutually agreed upon, will be a

---

[204]   SCHÖNSLEBEN, 2000, p. 61.

[205]   HINES ET AL., 1997.

[206]   VON WREDE, 2000.

[207]   Additionally, the big SCM software vendors offer strategy opportunity assessment, e.g., with the i2 value proposition which results in an estimate of operational improvements (see www.i2.com/valueprop/ (August 2001)).

very helpful tool. While using the various techniques for analyzing supply chains, a profound knowledge of the current state-of-the-art in the logistics network is gained. Hence, a first high-level generic transcorporate performance measurement (self)assessment of the As-Is state can be undertaken to help set new targets for the To-Be state and give rough directions for the subsequent action plans. Based on our experiences, the graphical representation of the generic key performance indicators, the so-called SCORcard level o metrics, serves as an easy-to-use and powerful tool[208].

For each of the logistics performance indicators defined above, the participants must identify the current logistics network capabilities and identify the performance required to deliver the selected SCM strategy. Therefore, in figure 6-5, the solid area describes the As-Is state, whereas the dashed line symbolizes the To-Be stage as a result of the logistics network analysis. This gap analysis provides the means for setting achievable targets for the following improvement phase.

However, up to this phase, only first and second level managers have been engaged, and sustainable supply chain changes will not happen unless the wider workforce is involved. Now it is important to widen the supply chain project team. By this point, the management team will have an idea of the direction and possible areas that could be addressed. However, this information has not come from the 'doers' in the organization who are involved in the day-to-day information and physical flow. The bottom-up detailed analysis should, therefore, be done by a team of doers, led by a manager who understands these activities. Finally, when designing new process organizations, this will ensure bottom-up buy-in through the developed improvement plans from the wider team.

- *Phase of improvements:*

Once the detailed analysis is completed, supply chain teams will have gathered a great deal of information. People involved will then need to turn this into workable plans over a reasonable timeframe. After developing plans throughout the logistics network, the plans should be rolled out to ensure integration and alignment among the network entities. The output of this step should be a conceptual design of process organization as well as IT support for each partner of the logistics network to achieve supply chain excellence in the three performance target areas of collaboration, coordination and transformability. According to our findings, particularly the definition of the new responsibilities in the logistics network (e.g., inventory levels and ownership, information sharing etc.) is one of the most difficult topics to solve collaboratively.

- *Phase of performance measurement:*

In the final phase of the integral model, the monitoring of the current logistics performance as well as highlighting the progress through a common supply chain initiative are in focus. Performance reviews must be conducted in the individual organizations with related review mechanisms, such as quarterly

---

[208]   Similar graphical representation of key success factors for change management can be found in HAFEN, 2000.

reports. At the beginning, the proposed generic SCORcard level 0 is a well-suited visualization tool to communicate the 'supply chain scores' between the partners. Additionally, if the partnership within the logistics network matures over time during the common supply chain initiative, the modification process can lead to additional selection of aggregated performance indicators of SCOR level 1 metrics towards a even more result-oriented perspective (e.g., costs). This was proven as an appropriate approach because all supply chain improvements should finally result in the desired better financial performance (e.g., total inventory reduction, total supply chain costs, etc.). Based on the results of performance evaluation, modifications might be necessary, which will lead to the respective phase of the model depending on the achieved performance results.

	Aggregated level 1 metrics	Disadvantage	Average or median	Advantage	Best-in-class
Delivery performance & quality	Delivery performance	◼ 55%	69%		93%
	Fill rate by line item	79% ◼	88%		97%
	Order fulfillment lead time		225 Days ◼	200 Days	135 Days
Flexibility & responsive-ness	Perfect order fulfillment	◼ 65.7%	65.7%		92.4%
	Supply chain response time		225 Days	110 Days ◼	72 Days
	Upside production flexibility		22 Days	◼ 15 Days	9 Days
Cost	Supply chain Mgt cost	16.4% ◼	14.4%		8.6%
	Warranty cost as % of revenue	2.9% ◼	2.4%		1.2 %
	Value added per employee		$ 139K	◼ $ 150K	$ 275K
Assets	Inventory days of supply	92 Days ◼	84 Days		55 Days
	Cash-to-cash cycle time	◼ 120 Days	99.4 Days		35.6 Days
	Asset turns		1.7 Turns	◼ 2.8 Turns	4.7 Turns

Source: Supply chain scorecard of version 3.1   ◼ Score of network

Figure 6-6:   Potential aggregated performance indicators 'SCORcard level 1'

In conclusion, it is also important to know that these four phases of the model are flexible guidelines, which must be applied according to the needs of the logistics network rather than fixed, predefined process steps. For example, if a detailed common understanding of the network already exists, the starting point of the initiative will be certainly phase 2. Furthermore, based on the results of the collaborative performance measurement in phase 4, it could be also necessary to go through phase 2 and 3 again or could even lead to a complete (re)configuration of the existing logistics network, which would lead to the initiating phase 1, marked by the arrows in figure 6-3.

6.4   Final remarks on the proposed integral model for performance measurement

The proposed integral model for performance measurement in logistics networks encompasses a two-phase approach (see figure 6-1). In the first phase, high-level generic performance indicators will be reported *(Enablers)* and in a second phase, those indicators can be enlarged by aggregation and transformation of current performance indicators in place on a network level based on the degree of openness and trust within the logistics network *(Results)*.

To summarize all key characteristics of the new integral model, proposed as an enhancement of the current SCOR model, table 17 (compare also section 5.3) will be used. This will also help to demonstrate the main differences to the already existing approaches.

Key requirements for collaborative performance measurement	Key features of new model for collaborative performance measurement
Network-oriented	PLAN Supply chain: transcorporate process demands as the first step, the modeling and configuration of the network including all respective partners
Partnership-oriented	The new identified performance target areas with the assigned indicators ('Enabler') must be evaluated collaboratively in the first step
Balanced approach	The mix of qualitative and quantitative performance indicators is given and must be determined by the needs of the partners themselves
Business process-oriented	The basis of the new model is a business process view of the logistics network, promoted by the implementation guidelines
Multi-level-oriented	Based on the degree of partnership and the participating units, the proposed model can be extended towards the required level of detail (top-down approach)
Model-oriented	Systematic guidelines are provided on how to set up a collaborative performance measurement
Scope-oriented	The proposed set of metrics (Enabler as well as Results) can be tailor-made to the specific needs of the logistics network

Table 17:   Key characteristics of new proposed integral model

This is an iterative approach and based on the intensity of partnership in the network, and thus more and more information and metrics will be shared. However, the starting point will be the generic performance indicators. This assures that all partners do not have to disclose sensitive information (e.g., financial data, internal performance metrics) at the beginning of a collaboration. Furthermore, at the beginning, mainly the top management is involved, so that at this time the more fundamental and strategic decisions related to the direction of further collaboration can be defined. During the maturation of the network, more and more participants will share their information to contribute to an integral model of performance measurement on a network level. In addition, as several authors in the research area of performance measurement have partly shown (see HOLMBERG 2000, GUNASEKARAN ET AL. 2001, VAN HOEK 1998), this proposed set of performance indicators for transcorporate logistics supports and contributes to a comprehensive integral view of a logistics network.

The new integral model is very much partnership-oriented, the high-level generic performance indicators, especially, strive for a common evaluation of the efficiency of collaboration, coordination, and transformability from a network perspective. In addition, using the recommended two-phase approach, the balance of enabling and result-oriented performance indicators can be determined by the network members themselves. This is one of the big advantages of the model, not to strive for financial key performance indicators (e.g., network ROi) at the beginning of a common performance measurement approach. Furthermore, through the recommended process steps, the performance measurement can be easily adapted with respect to scope and partners, based on the needs of the network (e.g., if results recommend a new (re)configuration). According to the process-orientation of the entire model and the recommended guidelines, integral logistics planning as well as execution will be efficiently supported in a systematic manner. In addition, through the enhancement of the current SCOR model, the concept of a hierarchical approach can be continuously supported as well.

In conclusion, this integral model provides a complete set of performance indicators and systematic implementation guidelines upon which a logistics network performance can be assessed and finally leads the way towards the global optimum of logistics network.

7

7 Case studies

The following two case studies demonstrate how the proposed integral model (see figure 6-1) for performance measuring in logistics networks, consisting of top-level generic logistics network performance indicators and assigned enabling process elements (see figure 6.3), can be applied in industry. Both initiatives are results within the CTI project ProNet,[209] which contributed to a great extent to the proposed integral model, on the one hand for the validation of appropriate generic performance indicators as well as on the other for the definition of suitable process elements to support the proposed model.

In the following, the collaboratively initiated supply chain improvements as well as respective expected benefits will be highlighted[210].

In addition, these cases are structured according to the four major phases of a supply chain initiative based on a common performance measurement approach (see figure 6-3), to demonstrate the time development of such an improvement project as well as to reveal the necessary identified steps in industrial practice.

7.1 CASE A: Huber+Suhner AG

In this case study, supply chain coordination excellence in daily operations within the existing logistics network of Huber+Suhner AG, a large, multi-unit organi-

---

[209] Funded by the Swiss Commission for Technology and Innovation (CTI), contract-No. 4209 and 4674.1.

[210] Unfortunately, the detailed analysis results cannot be presented (e.g., SCORcard level 0), in order to guarantee the non-disclosure of confidential company information.

zation, was the main performance target area to be addressed by the collaborative supply chain initiative.

7.1.1   The configuration of the logistics network

At present, the HUBER+SUHNER group employs 4200 people worldwide and is operating several production facilities, warehouses and sales organizations all over the world. The headquarters is located in Herisau and Pfäffikon/Zurich, Switzerland, and its consolidated net sales exceeded CHF 700 million in 1999. The group mainly acts on an international scale indicatedby the continuous increase of exports, which reached 80% in 2000. With subsidiaries in Germany, Great Britain, France, Sweden, United States, Canada, Australia, Hong Kong, Singapore, China, Sweden, Brazil and sales agencies in more than 50 countries, the HUBER+SUHNER group delivers products in the area of telecommunication technologies, energy transmission and materials technology to demanding niche markets. It is worth mentioning that particularly the telecommunications and the automotive industry lead the way in supply chain management and therefore, the following supply chain initiative and improvement efforts focus mainly on these industry sections. Figure 7-1 demonstrates the rough configuration of the logistics network with its source, make, and deliver entities.

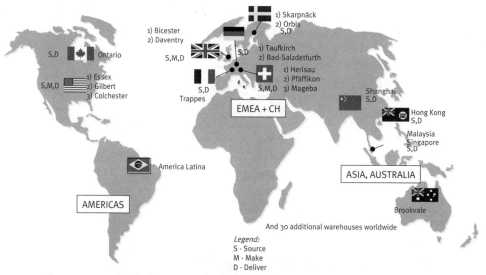

Figure 7-1:   Logistics network of HUBER+SUHNER AG

For the following supply chain initiative, only a part of the entire logistics network served as an supply chain exemplar.

7.1.2   The analysis of the logistics network

The HUBER+SUHNER group is currently in a transition state from a 'strategic' network organization, based on traditional buyer/supplier relationships and central control exercised by the headquarters towards a supply chain network organization[211]. This significant transition could be well recorded and communicated to all partners with the aid of the identified characteristic features of logistics networks (see tables 8, 9, and 10) in order to ensure a common understanding about the new challenging logistics network requirements. In figure 7-2, the main characteristic features of the analyzed part of HUBER+SUHNER's logistics network are monitored, which gave a first rough description of the key network dimensions as well as a common agreed-upon communication base for further supply chain initiatives of HUBER+SUHNER.

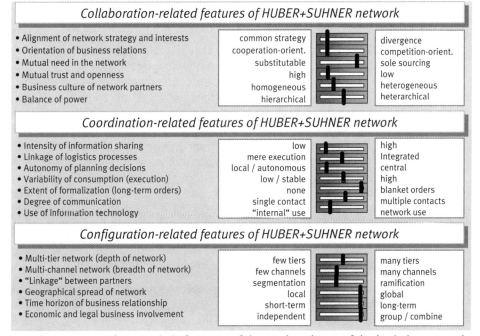

Figure 7-2:   Characteristic features of the analyzed part of the logistics network

In the following, some of the key features of the analyzed part of the network will be pointed out:

- In the *dimension of collaboration*, high supply chain strategic alignment, the similar business culture and values as well as a high amount of trustful relationship could be recorded.

- Furthermore, in the *dimension of coordination*, the network partners commonly agreed on the characteristic features of limited information sharing

---

[211]   HIEBER/ALARD/BOXLER, 2001, p. 78.

practice on a network level as well as IT use mainly for supporting internal business processes.

- Finally, within the *dimension of configuration*, long and stable business relations between the partners, the global scale, and the high economic and legal business dependence according to the selected internal network of the HUBER+SUHNER group have to be noted.

In addition to this first rough analysis, specific transcorporate logistics issues in the area of information availability (e.g., for the purpose of tracking and tracing or balancing demand and supply on a network level), information straight-through processing (e.g., multiple data re-entering), data replications (e.g., multiple part numbers) as well as non-standardization of data formats could been identified by further analysis of global key accounts[212, 213]. In particular, transparency of inventory level of finished goods information has been one of the main concerns and it was chosen as the first task in the following supply chain initiative.

The conducted analyses have shown that the relevant network organizations of HUBER+SUHNER, subsidiaries as well as the headquarters itself, could not directly mutually access the information concerning the inventory levels of one product item, either on the level of 'final assembly' or 'component', stocked in several different geographical locations within the network of HUBER+SUHNER. As a matter of fact, it was not possible to monitor the inventory levels on a network level in order to balance it in an optimal way and allocate best global demand to local supply sites. For instance, because of the lack of inventory level information, it was possible that, even though the requested item was available at warehouse X, a new production order was generated and expedited in location Y.

At present, only remote accesses on the various different local ERP systems or extensive telephone calls could deliver this information. The results were high inventory levels at several locations and non-optimal production schedules, which led to unnecessary high utilization of production capacities.

To summarize these findings, the proposed high-level generic logistics network SCORcard (see figure 6-5) was used, which demonstrated the current logistics state on a network level in a comprehensive way. This tool served as an excellent means to communicate the necessary supply chain initiatives between HUBER+SUHNER partners as well as for setting the next supply chain direction.

7.1.3   Improvements and performance measurement in the logistics network

The uncovered need for improvements in the area of supply chain coordination excellence was monitored and communicated by the respective network perfor-

---

[212]   VILLARD, 2000.

[213]   HIEBER ET AL., 2001, p. 77.

mance indicators of information availability, organizational communication, and IT support on the network level resulted in the initiative of Supply Chain Inventory Visibility (SCIV). Under this concept, HUBER+SUHNER is striving for the visualization of information in real time to support transcorporate logistics activities (e.g., logistics planning decisions, tracking and tracing, exception detection and handling, and historical analysis). Related to better information availability, SCIV should finally lead to increased profitability, resulting from significant inventory reductions.

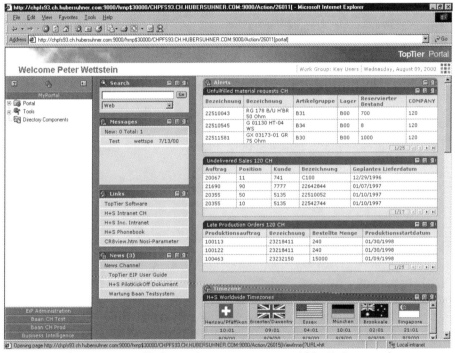

Figure 7-3:   *Concept of information transparency within H+S network*

To meet these new transcorporate logistics requirements, the idea of a common ERP/IT infrastructure based on a superior software level was created. For this purpose, several software products were evaluated and finally, the software supplier, named TopTier Software, Inc. selected. This product represents an enterprise information portal which allows the members of the logistics network direct access to the relevant information resources through the HyperRelational™ technology[214].

---

[214] TopTier Software Inc, founded in 1996, is located in San José, California. In 2001, it was acquired by SAP for $400 million. TopTier's HyperRelational technology places a layer of abstraction between users and enterprise systems by DRAG and RELATE via graphical user interfaces. Hence, several different 'data' sources can be linked to each other.

In the first step of this initiative, the issue of inventory visibility was addressed successfully as the following example of the preliminary study reveals (see figure 7-3).

The new IT support enables the network organizations of HUBER+SUHNER (in the preliminary study Switzerland, Great Britain, United States, Germany) to integrate several data sources in order to generate an optimal delivery and production plan by balancing global customer demand and local supplies on a network perspective. This will lead to better utilization of existing production capacities, lower inventory levels and better customer responsiveness.

Furthermore, as the figure shows, not only information related to inventory levels, but also alerts and exception reports of logistics states within the entire network can be shown. Based on the success of the first phase and the further huge potential of this technology, it is intended to enlarge the use towards even more comprehensive logistics information (e.g., production capacities) in a further step.

In the final phase of the integral model, by monitoring the relevant performance indicators in the area of supply chain coordination excellence on a regular basis, the onward significant improvements could be monitored and the ability to achieve the ambitious targeted logistics state in the near future has been completely proven.

7.1.4   Final comments

By the use of a 'transcorporate' IT infrastructure, HUBER+SUHNER could address the main issue of low information availability on a network level. By using this new software tool, the possibility for an efficient communication between the players in the logistics network is set. However, some prerequisites, mainly standardization activities between the network partners, must still be fulfilled in front, so that the proposed action plans will finally lead to the expected result (e.g., network-wide single part numbers, definition of transfer pricing to allow 'network' balancing of demand and supply). Furthermore, the transition of HUBER+SUHNER towards a supply chain organization must be further supported and promoted to reduce the apparent tension between 'network'-level coordination and 'local'-level optimization. Thus, an integrated performance measurement system will support solving this situation.

Furthermore, to maintain and enlarge the logistics knowledge as well as to make sustainable improvements, HUBER+SUHNER is currently building up a Corporate

Logistics Services[215] (CLS) program, which mainly strives for improvements in the area of supply chain transformability.

7.2   **CASE B: DiverseyLever AG**

In this case study, supply chain collaboration excellence within the logistics network of the DiverseyLever AG, including 'self-owned' network entities as well as third-party distributors, was the main performance target area to be addressed by the following supply chain initiative. Here, the main focus is on the transcorporate demand planning process, which should be transformed from a mainly divergent process to a highly integrated planning process.

7.2.1   The configuration of the logistics network

DiverseyLever AG, a subsidiary of the Unilever group, employs about 12,000 people worldwide, working in more than 60 countries. The main product groups are cleaning and hygiene systems with an approximately $1 billion annual turnover. The following supply chain initiative took place in the building care division, where mainly single disc machines, vacuum cleaners, and scrubber-dryers are produced. Its origin and the promoter of the following supply chain initiative came from the production facility in Münchwilen, Switzerland with approximately 100 employees. The DiverseyLever Group operates several national sales organizations in Europe as well as overseas, which independently manage their own regional warehouses. In addition, third-party distributors, which are offering DiverseyLever products, are also delivered by Münchwilen. Figure 7-4 shows the logistics network in a schematic way.

---

[215]   The implementation of Corporate Logistics Services (CLS) strives for achieving flexibilization of the H+S logistics and the establishment of an H+S-wide integral logistics management and adequate services network of Corporate Logistics Services. This is not a question of building up a new organization but of integrating the existing logistics services into a network and to further develop it into a concerted logistics services in cooperation with external partners of H+S.

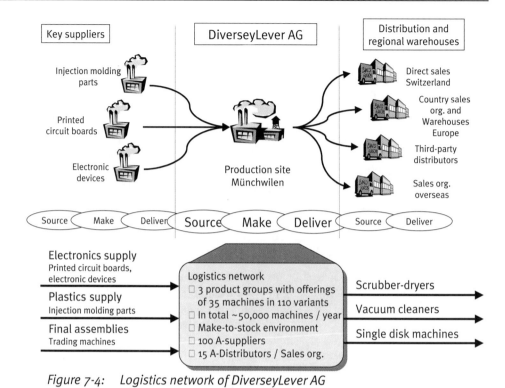

Figure 7-4:　Logistics network of DiverseyLever AG

7.2.2　The analysis of the logistics network

The transcorporate demand planning process has been a major issue over a long time period. At present, the demand planning is the responsibility of the country sales organizations and each organization is making its own 'national' forecast, supported by a common standard 'demand data' sheet[216]. Those are transferred on a regular basis from all relevant sales organizations (internal as well as external network entities) to the planner of the unique production facility in Münchwilen, Switzerland[217]. Here, the planner has to consolidate the figures and convert them into appropriate time segments, which then serve as the input for the local master production schedule.

Thus, the main issue in this demand planning process is the costly and time-consuming collection of data from the entire distribution network as well as the minimal possibility for collaboration between the network partners during the demand forecasting process steps (e.g., sharing of information of market developments, trends, etc.). Furthermore, first results of the supply chain

---

[216]　Common data gathering sheet based on Microsoft Excel to capture the independent demand of 'lead' machines of key sales organizations for a period of the next 12 months.

[217]　Besides a high-volume production facility for vacuum cleaners in China.

analysis revealed[218] that this non-integrated planning process resulted in a high variation of forecast qualities of the different sales organization. To cope with this issue, a high local safety buffer stock must be provided in Münchwilen to guarantee the high service level agreements, however, a lot of variance and disturbance is introduced in the supply chain by a poor quality forecast.

In a first step, by using the respective generic and aggregated logistics performance indicators (e.g., supply chain planning collaboration, degree of forecast qualities etc.) as well as the morphological scheme (see figure 7-5), the current state and performance of transcorporate logistics could be revealed and communicated between the network partners in general manner.

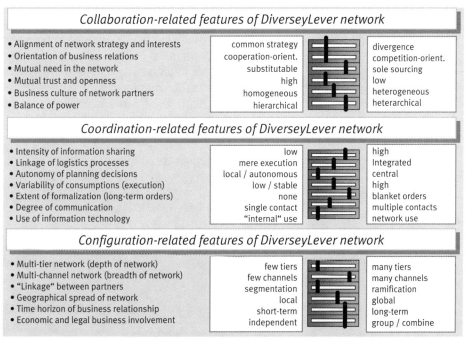

Figure 7-5:   Characteristic features of the analyzed part of the logistics network

7.2.3   Improvements in the logistics network

To achieve supply chain collaboration excellence in the transcorporate demand process, the concept of a web-based forecast information sharing platform has been generated, which will lead to a high degree of interaction between the forecast planners in the network and finally should lead to shorter and more frequent planning cycles (e.g., quick notice of exceptions) and finally to more accurate forecast data. Better forecast data in the short-term horizon, make it possible to define a frozen period within the rolling forecast sheets, to smooth

---

[218]   KOLATORSKI, 2001.

the entire material flow from the key suppliers, the single production facility, to the distribution and regional warehouses. As a matter of fact, this will significantly counteract the identified bullwhip effect.

Furthermore, by providing additional information on the web-based forecast platform for the sales organizations, for instance, information about market trends, sales history, demand data of relevant regions as well as order and delivery information (see figure 7-6), the quality of the collaborative demand planning process can be significantly supported.

The implementation of this new logistics information and forecasting platform is still in its design stage, but the underlying concept as well as a prototype of the potential web-based information platform can be seen in figure 7-6. The collaborative approach and early integration of the sales organizations especially (e.g., conducting of a survey about their needs of support in transcorporate forecast procedures) as well as guaranteeing more information for the sales organizations, the common supply chain initiative could be well originated. Here, the high-level performance indicators for communicating the current state of the logistics network and revealing the need for improvements were very useful, which will also be part of further common project reviews.

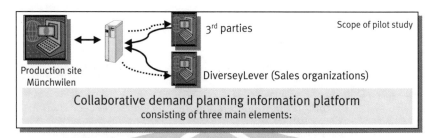

Figure 7-6:   Prototype of forecast information platform

In this supply chain initiative, the phase 4 'collaborative performance review on a regular basis' has not been reached yet.

7.2.4   Final remarks

In this case, the biggest obstacle of the supply chain initiative has been the collaboration between the various levels in the DiverseyLever logistics network and uncovering the need for and the potential of an improved transcorporate demand planning process. Thus, by demonstrating the interrelationships and dynamics in supply chains (e.g., common supply chain training sessions[219] with the sales organizations), the necessity for a higher degree of collaborative planning as well as the commitment to put more effort in the demand planning cycle process could be shown. As a further step, by implementing the high-level performance indicators, this collaborative approach should now be established on a regular basis to guarantee that the current high level of collaboration can be maintained.

---

[219]   Especially in this case, the use of the logistics game, the 'Beer-game', developed by MIT, was a powerful tool in achieving a common understanding and significant learning effects.

8

8 Conclusions and outlook

8.1 Summary

As the findings of this research indicate, there is an extensive need for new approaches to collaborative performance measurement in logistics network to support transcorporate logistics. Therefore, the main objective of this work was to evaluate current approaches of performance measurement regarding their applicability in a supply chain management context and to make a contribution to support improvements in transcorporate logistics.

Among the main issues identified were the isolated optimization in logistics networks supported by current performance measurements, the weak link between the performance indicators and network logistics management practice, and the predominate reliance on short-term operational performance indicators (see table 13). It was also argued in this work that the existing approaches support corporate performance measurements well, but they cannot be simply transferred and applied on a network level. Hence, seven key principles on performance measurement in logistics network were presented based upon the new integral model that was developed (see section 6-2).

This research goes beyond the previous work of performance measurement and introduces an integral model consisting of generic and aggregated performance indicators as well as implementation guidelines dedicated to improving performance across the entire logistics network. The proposed model consists of three main elements (see figure 6-1 and 6-3):

- Generic high-level performance indicators in phase 1 – *Enablers*
- Aggregated corporate performance indicators in phase 2 – *Results*
- Basic implementation guidelines on how to apply and succeed in a collaborative performance measurement – *Process steps*

According to our research, the most advanced tool in the area of logistics performance measurement is the existing SCOR model, which served as the basis for the new integral model (see figures 6-2 and 6-4), which supports the proposed collaborative, network-oriented performance measurement approach.

By combining the two sets of performance indicators *(Enablers and Results)* with the related proposed process steps, a powerful tool is provided for an integral performance measurement approach for logistics networks, which form a comprehensive framework upon which a logistics network performance can be (self)assessed.

In addition, as the partnership matures, more and more performance indicators, also from the corporate performance measurement already in place, can be included, which can finally lead to a commonly agreed-upon performance measurement of the logistics network.

In addition, by providing characteristic features of logistics networks (see chapter 4), the baseline for benchmarking of logistics networks is set. According to those features, similar network types can be identified, which then allow a direct comparison.

Furthermore, the recommended integral model as well as process steps can be tailored to the specific needs of the logistics network. That means, it is also reasonable to look only at specific phases or performance target area of the proposed integral framework. Furthermore, case studies have proven that the proposed integral model can contribute to a significant degree to an efficient supply chain management.

In summary, the proposed, two-phase integral model encompasses generic and aggregated performance indicators to provide the involved network entities with input that identifies areas for improvements from a network perspective, and allows them to direct management attention to those network entities with high potential for improvement.

8.2   Limitations and gained experiences

In this section, a rough evaluation of the proposed methodology and experiences gained by applying this methodology will be pointed out. In the following, the main pitfalls are mentioned:

- *Motivation and participation of all key players*

In general, as already revealed in chapter 4, the central prerequisite of all supply chain initiatives are open, trustful, cooperation-oriented business relationships.

As soon as one key player of the network does not cooperate, the entire approach has to be questioned. However, this is seldom the case because the benefits of collaborative business relationships are more and more well-known and proven by numerous case studies in industry.

- *Potential conflict areas of local vs. global interests*

There will be still potential conflict areas of local vs. global interests. However, by the collaborative approach and the proposed generic performance indicators, the model will help to detect these conflict areas at a very early stage and can help to overcome those in a structured manner using the proposed guidelines.

- *Scope of supply chain projects*

One of the biggest hurdles of supply chain projects is the effort and scope of such projects. As soon as several organizations have to set up a project organization, the time frame and expenditure enlarge significantly. Especially in the geographical dispersions of globally acting network organizations, this can often lead to a reduction of the project team to a fraction of the actual necessary size. Experiences have also shown that as soon as a 'local' problem area emerges, the priority of the global issue will be pushed in the background.

- *Establishing changes in transcorporate organizational structures and routines*

Most of the projects recommend changes in the transcorporate structure and processes as well as the need for 'manpower' commitment to maintain the new routines, which, for example, results in the fact that the review organization must be set up or some supply chain performance indicators may not be currently measured. However, supply chains are typically comprised of many independent value-adding partners who have control and the financial responsibility for their portion of the network. But how to initiate changes if no central responsibility or control is in place and the problem area lies outside of a company's domain of influence? In particular, the proposed collaborative approach can deliver a major element in overcoming this issue.

A transformation towards supply chain management and collaborative performance measurement will take time, a lot of effort and commitment, but it will be worth the effort as several case studies have proven.

8.3   Recommendations for further research activities

As revealed in this work, particularly legal and economically independent enterprises closely integrated in a logistics network need new ways and approaches to a collaborative supply chain management. The practices and proposed new model in this work are considered 'leading edge' in many organizations in that they have only begun to be developed within the last several years. Even the cases described in the last chapter represent the organization's initial attempts at supply chain management and are in the process of being improved today.

Furthermore, the very nature of supply chain management is unique. Because of the incredible complexity and scale involved in managing the flow of goods and information between multiple entities in the supply chain, there exists a broad and ever-changing set of priorities, which will require a level of responsiveness never encountered before in the business world[220].

Thus, by analyzing the potential future developments in the industrial environment, the strong impression can be gained that this will lead to even more integrated and complex supply chain partnerships in logistics networks. Therefore, by establishing the basis for a collaborative performance measurement with this work, some fundamental recommendations and guidelines are proposed for facing these new challenges. In addition, this section explores some of the further research areas to be addressed to support sustainable collaborative supply chain management.

These include the following:

- Information and communication technologies
- Sharing risks in transcorporate logistics
- Empirical evaluation of interdependencies of performance indicators on a network perspective

Information and communication technologies

The spread of information and communication technology will increase more and more and will become the major enabler for realizing an integrated logistics network. However, one of the major weaknesses of traditional SCM software tools is the lack of a collaborative planning and execution support between the network partners. As a matter of fact, especially for the identified supply chain network organizations, efficient IT support at reasonable costs for supply chain management is not offered yet, even though most of the SCM software vendors claim this fact. Even though fascinating technology in terms of the World Wide Web is available, proprietary SCM software applications are still promoted for supply chain management. But, as revealed in chapter 4, most of the network entities are integrated not only in one network with one unified software application, but also in several other networks with numerous different software packages, and the company does not want to "sign on" every system. In addition, the support of the decision-making process of current SCM software applications is still very centralized and does not contribute to a collaborative planning and execution in the logistics network. As soon as there is no longer an inequity of power existing in the logistics network, such concepts will no longer succeed. New and innovative ways must be developed, which allow a collaborative interaction between the network partners in an simple way.

---

[220] HANDFIELD, 1999, p. 153.

Sharing risks in transcorporate logistics

In order to function in such an integrated collaborative way, entities in the logistics network will need to know more about one another. To manage the flow of goods and information, organizations will need to share both strategic-level information (regarding corporate and business unit strategies, market developments, etc.) as well as operational-level information (number of orders, pricing policies, market forecast, etc.)[221]. Furthermore, as closer integration into the logistics network evolves, investment in an efficient information technology infrastructure will be required to master the necessary degree of network integration. Thus, as companies become more and more dependent on their logistics network members, they will have to find new and innovative ways to manage the risks associated with sharing proprietary and sensitive information as well as to clarify the split of common investments and the resulting benefits.

Empirical evaluation of the interdependencies of performance indicators from a network perspective

In particular, further suggestions for research should be primarily directed at developing a better understanding of the dependence between performance indicators of the different proposed SCOR levels. For instance, the dependencies between the high-level generic performance indicators as well as the cause and effect relations between the key performance metrics of SCOR level 1 and the more diagnostics metrics on the subsequent hierarchical levels of SCOR, as the new SCOR version 5.0 is already promising.

Therefore, in relation to the results of this work, further empirical investigations are recommended. Especially in those based on the identified specific network patterns spanned by the logistics characteristic features, network specific benchmark data should be collected and evaluated to identify the best-in-class network performance. In this area, more research is needed in order to support significantly the development of collaborative logistics networks. First research projects (e.g., IMS EU project PRODCHAIN) are already on their way to investigating and solving these issues.

---

[221]   HANDFIELD, 1999, p. 155.

Appendix A: Performance Dimension at network level

Term	Type	Definition	From process category/ Element #:
Supply chain collaboration efficiency	Performance dimension	The ability to work together and act collaboratively in a win-win partnership to fulfill (final) customer demand in a logistics network. All activities should be oriented towards the global optimum of the logistics network.	P0
Supply chain coordination efficiency	Performance dimension	The ability of logistics network partners to coordinate and communicate efficiently in daily operations. That means that organizations, people, and systems all have access to relevant logistics information regardless of organization, location or company.	P0
Supply chain transform-ability	Performance dimension	The ability to achieve a high substantial potential of flexibility in (re)configuration of supply chains between the partners in the network by means of practicing and sharing logistics know-how, capabilities, routines, and skills as well as leveraging ideas and visions.	P0

Table 18:   Performance dimensions at level 0

Appendix B: Performance METRICS at network level

Term	Type	Definition	Examples of factors of influence (soft and hard factors)
Performance target area of supply chain collaboration excellence			
Supply chain strategic alignment	Metric	The amount of common network-directed efforts and focus towards collaborative, integrated management of the logistics network to achieve overall optimum of the entire network	– Common set of targets and objectives – Common investments in network resources (e.g., common material, capacitiy or IT resources) – Common agreements on: – Quick time-to-market for new products, – Quality expectations, – Target market segments, – Expected volumes, – Pricing, – Desired overall growth rate of network, – Efforts towards technological capability consistent with partners
Supply chain planning collaboration	Metric	Degree of collaborative planning that results in common logistics planning activities (e.g., CPFR concepts) based on significant insights in planning routines and results	– Amount of collaborative planning routines (e.g., CPFR) – Degree of interaction between planning activities – Planning process cycle time – Number and frequency of plan updates between partners – Simultaneous engineering
Supply chain execution collaboration	Metric	Degree of collaborative execution that results in common logistics execution activities based on significant insights in execution routines	– Amount of collaborative execution routines (e.g., VMI, Cont. Replenishment) – Degree of interaction between execution activities – Percent of demand/supply on VMI/CRP-programs – Common designed activities for expediting, alerts or exception handling

Table 19:   Performance METRICS assigned to SCOR level 0 (I/II)

Term	Type	Definition	Examples of factors of influence (soft and hard factors)
Performance target area of supply chain Coordination excellence			
Supply chain organizational communication	Metric	The amount of communication and formal contacts between the participating network partners in daily logistics operations	– Common 'language' in place (e.g., SCOR model) – Communication channels used (e.g., 'supply chain manager') – Number of on-site visits – Supply chain openness and trust – Number of 'network' events (e.g., supplier days)
Supply chain information availability	Metric	The degree of information access that should enable everyone in the network to get the most useful and up-to-date information as required for logistics planning and execution processes in daily operations	– Degree of available-to-promise (ATP) capabilities – % of POS data availability – % of information availability related to: – Forecasts – Inventory levels – Capacities – Order tracking and tracing
Supply chain IT support	Metric	The degree of IT support for transcorporate logistics planning and execution in daily operations	– Transcorporate planning support (e.g., SCM software application) – Transcorporate execution support (e.g., number of online order lines – EDI transaction) – Transcorporate Information Data Warehouse – Communication between IT systems (respectively, # of media breaks) – Transcorporate Internet activities (e.g., network information portal)

Table 20:   Performance METRICS assigned to SCOR level 0 (II/III)

Term	Type	Definition	Examples of factors of influence (soft and hard factors)
Performance target area of supply chain transformability Flexibility			
Supply chain know-how	Metric	The ability to practice best-of-breed supply chain management and to define logistics standards for the logistics network	– Supply chain logistics audits – Benchmarking position – Patents and logistics prizes awarded – APICS trained personnel – Knowledge of best practices of SCM activities
Supply chain skill sharing	Metric	The ability to transfer specific logistics skills to other network members and to share logistics knowledge based on continuous learning	– Exchange of employees – Common project reviews – Definition of transcorporate logistics guidelines – Network teaching activities – Number of continuous improvement suggestions from transcorporate network members
Supply chain (re)configu-ration flexibility	Metric	The time required to define and achieve a new configuration of a supply chain for a new or a sustainable change of existing product (the rapidity with which these changes can be accomplished)	– New product time-to-market (end-product level) – New product time-to-first make (first-product level)

Table 21:   Performance METRICS assigned to SCOR level 0 (III/II)

Appendix C: Performance METRICS at SCOR level 1

Term	Type	Definition	From process category/Element #:
Asset turns	Metric	Total gross product revenue ÷ Total net assets	M1, M1.3, M1.4, M2, M2.3, M2.4, M3, M3.4, M3.5
Cash-to-cash cycle time	Metric	Cash-to-cash cycle time = inventory days of supply + days sales outstanding – average payment period for materials (time it takes for a dollar to flow back into a company after its been spent for raw materials). For services, this represents the time from the point where a company pays for the resources consumed in the performance of a service to the time that the company received payment from the customer for those services.	P1, M1.2, M2.2, M3.3, D2.12, D3.11
Cost of goods sold	Metric	The cost associated with buying raw materials and producing finished goods. This cost includes direct costs (labor, materials) and indirect costs (overhead).	All
Delivery performance	Metric	The percentage of orders that are fulfilled on or before the customer's requested date.	EP.1, P1, P1.3, P4, P4.3, P4.4, M1, M2, M3, D1.10, D2, D2.9, D3, D1.3, D3.8
Fill rates	Metric	The percentage of ship-from-stock orders shipped within 24 hours of order receipt. For services, this metric is the proportion for services that are filled so that the service is completed within 24 hours	P1, P1.3, P4, P4.4, M1.3, D1, D1.3, D1.9, D2
Inventory days of supply	Metric	Total gross value of inventory at standard cost before reserves for excess and obsolescence. Only includes inventory on company books, future liabilities should not be included. Five point annual average of the sum of all gross inventories (raw materials & WIP, plant FG, field FG, field samples, other; COGS 365).	EP.1, P1, P1.3, S1, S2, S3, M1.1, M2.1, M3.2

Table 22:   Performance METRICS assigned to SCOR level 1 (I/II)

Order fulfillment lead times	Metric	The average actual lead times consistently achieved, from customer signature/authorization to order receipt, order receipt to order entry complete, order entry complete to start-build, start build to order ready for shipment, order ready for shipment to customer receipt of order, and customer receipt of order to installation complete.	M3, M3.1, D1, D2, D3
Perfect order fulfillment	Metric	A 'perfect order' is defined as an order that meets all of the following standards: Delivered complete; all items on order are delivered in the quantities requested. Delivered on time to customer's request date, using your customer's definition of on-time delivery. Documentation supporting the order including packing slips, bills of lading, invoices, etc., is complete and accurate. Perfect condition: Faultlessly installed (as applicable), correct configuration, customer-ready, no damage.	D1.10, D1.11, D2, D2.2, D2.9, D2.10, D3, D3.8, D3.9
Production flexibility	Metric	Upside flexibility: The number of days required to achieve an unplanned sustainable 20% increase in production. Downside flexibility: The percentage order reduction sustainable at 30 days prior to delivery with no inventory or cost penalties.	M1.1, M2.1, M3.2
Supply chain response time[222]	Metric	The time at which a supply chain responds to marketplace changes	P1
Total supply chain management costs	Metric	Total logistics costs are the sum of supply-chain related MIS, finance and planning, inventory carrying, material acquisition, and order management costs.	EP.1, EP.2, EP.3, EP.4, EP.5, EP.6, EP.7, EP.8, EP.9, E.10, P4
Value-added productivity	Metric	Value added per employee is calculated as total product revenue less total material purchases total employment (in full-time equivalents).	P1, M1, M1.3, M2, M2.3, M3, M3.4
Warranty/returns processing costs	Metric	Warranty costs include materials, labor and problem diagnosis for product defects.	M1, M1.3, M1.4, M2, M2.3, M2.4, M3, M3.4, M3.5

Table 23:   Performance METRICS assigned to SCOR level 1 (II/II)

---

[222]   No definition in current SCOR version 4.0 available – this definition is based on the SCOR Version 4.0 change notes, but not an 'official' SCOR definition.

Appendix D: PROCESS category at network level

Term	Type	Definition	Process Category/ Element #:
Plan supply chain: trans- corporate	Process Category	The process of designing and controlling the supply chain in its entirely, consisting of all respective supply chains. In addition, to establish courses of action for performance measurement as well as identifying areas for improvement in collaboration.	P0
Supply chain initialization and configuration	Process Element	The process of identifying, selecting, and configuring, as a whole with network entities, all respective elements of a logistics network in the delivery of a product or service to the final customer.	P0.1
Supply chain analysis	Process Element	The process of analyzing, identifying, and prioritizing, as a whole with network entities, all respective elements of a logistics network in the delivery of a product or service to the final customer.	P0.2
Supply chain improvement	Process Element	The process of considering, and designing, as a whole with network entities, all respective elements of a logistics network in the delivery of a product or service to the final customer.	P0.3
Supply chain performance measurement	Process Element	The process of controlling, as a whole with network entities, all respective elements of a logistics network in the delivery of a product or service to the final customer.	P0.4

Table 24:   PROCESS category at level 0

Bibliography

ALARD, R., HIEBER, R. (2000): Lösungen für unternehmensübergreifende Kooperationen. Supply Chain Management und Business-to-Business Commerce. In: PPS Management 5 (2000) 2, pp. 10–14.

AMERICAN MANAGEMENT ASSOCIATION (1960): Executive Committee Charts – a description of the Du Pont Chart system for appraising operation performance, in AMA Management Bulletin June 1960, pp. 1–23.

AMR (2000): Application Spending and Penetration by Vertical Market, 2001–2002, The Market Aanalysis and Review Series, AMR Research, Boston.

APICS (1998): Dictionary, 9th Edition, APICS, Alexandria, Virginia.

APICS (2000a): Instructor Guide, Detailed Scheduling and Planning, Session 8: Establishing Relationships with Suppliers, APICS, Alexandria, Virginia.

APICS (2000b): Instructor Guide, Detailed Scheduling and Planning, Session 9: Supplier Relationships and Procurement Plans, APICS, Alexandria, Virginia.

AXELROD, R. (1984): The Evolution of Co-operation, Basic Books, New York.

BALLING, R. (1997): Kooperation – Strategische Allianzen, Netzwerke, Joint-Ventures und andere Organisationsformen zwischenbetrieblicher Zusammenarbeit in Theorie und Praxis, Frankfurt, Lang.

BECHTEL, C., JAYARAM, J (1997): Supply Chain Management: A Strategic Perspective. International Journal of Logistics Management, Vol. 8, No. 1, pp. 15–34.

BOUTELLIER, R., GIRSCHIK, S. (2001): Trilaterale Beziehungskonstellationen in der Automobilindustrie, io Management, Nr. 1/2, pp. 18–24.

BOX, G., HUNTER, W., HUNTER, J. (1978): Statistics for Experiments – An Introduction to Design, Data Analysis, and Model Building, John Wiley & Sons, New York.

CHRISTOPHER, M. (1998): Logistics and Supply Chain Management – Strategies for Reducing Cost and Improving Service, Financial Times, Pitman Publisher, 1998.

COASE, R.H. (1937): The Nature of the Firm, in: Economica: 4, 1937, pp. 386–405.

COASE, R. H. (1988): The Firm, the Market, and the Law, University of Chicago Press, Chicago and London.

ELLRAM, L. M., COOPER, M. C. (1990): Supply Chain Management, Partnerships and the Shipper-Third Party Relationship, The International Journal of Logistics Management, Vol. 1, No. 2 (1990), pp. 1–10.

ELLRAM, L. (1991): Supply Chain Management – the industrial organization perspective, International Journal of Physical Distribution & Logistics Management, Vol. 21, No. 1, 1991, pp. 13–22.

FACETT, S.E., CLINTON, S. (1996): Enhancing logistics performance to improve the competitiveness of mfg org., Production & Inventory Management Journal 37, No. 1, pp. 40–46.

FRIGO-MOSCA, F., ALBERTI, G. E. (1995): Advanced Logistic Partnership: an Agile Concept for Equitable Relationships between Buyers and Suppliers, Proceedings of the 1995 World Symposium of Integrated Manufacturing, APICS, Auckland NZ, March 1995, pp. 31–35.

GUNASEKARAN, A., PATEL, C., TIRTIROGLU, E. (2001): Performance Measures and Metrics in a Supply Chain Environment, International Journal of Operations & Production Management, Vol. 21, No. 1/2, 2001, pp. 71–87.

HAFEN, U. (1999): Ansätze zur nachhaltigen Reorganisation in der Unternehmenslogistik von kleinen und mittleren Unternehmen (KMU). Diss. Techn. Wiss. ETH Zürich, Nr. 13093.

HAFERMALZ, O. (1976): Schriftliche Befragung – Möglichkeiten und Grenzen, Gabler Verlag, Wiesenbaden.

HANDFIELD, R., NICHOLS, E. (1999): Introduction to Supply Chain Management, Prentice-Hall.

HANDFIELD, R., KRAUSE, D., SCANNEL, T., MONCZKA, R. (2000): Avoid the Pitfalls, Sloan Management Review, Winter 2000, pp. 37–49.

HARRINGTON, L. (1995): Logistics, Agent for Change: Shaping the Integrated Supply Chain, Transportation and Distribution Management, Vol. 36, No. 1 (1995), pp. 30–34.

HEWITT, F. (1994): Supply Redesign, The International Journal of Logistics Management, Vol. 5, No. 2 (1994), pp. 1–9.

HIEBER, M. (2000): Recycling Networks: An Interdisciplinary Approach for Downcycling, Recycling and Upcycling, Seventeenth Conference of the Irish Manufacturing Committee 2000, IMC-17, NUI, Galway.

HIEBER, R. (1998): Optimierung von Produktionsnetzwerken durch Anwendung unternehmensübergreifender Diagnosetechnik. In: Industrie Management 6/1998, pp. 62–65.

HIEBER, R. (1999): Standard Software Applications for Supply Chain Management; Proceedings Euroma99 – Managing Operations Networks, 7th–8th June, 1999, Venice, Italy, pp. 245–251.

HIEBER, R, ALARD, R. (2000): Network Integration Using Advanced IT. In: Renchu Gan (Hrsg.): Information Technology for Business Management, 16th World Computer Congress 2000, August 21–25, 2000, Beijing, China, pp. 681–687.

HIEBER, R. (2000): Efficient Information Sharing for Supply Chain Management Networks. In: K. S. Taraman (Hrsg.): Pacific Conference on Manufacturing 2000, September 6th–8th, 2000, Detroit, USA, pp. 265–270.

HIEBER, R., WINDISCHER, A., ALARD, R., FISCHER, D. (2000): Erfolgreich kooperieren in Supply Chains – Trends und Praktiken in der unternehmensübergreifenden Zusammenarbeit, ETH-Zentrum für Unternehmenswissenschaft, August 2000.

HIEBER, R., ALARD, R., BOXLER, O. (2001): Einsatz neuer Software-Generation im Supply Chain Management – Gestaltung unternehmensübergreifender IT-Logistiknetzwerke, io Management 1/2 2001, pp. 72–80.

HIEBER, R., HARTEL, I., BURKHALTER, J.P.: Supporting the beer-game by the simultaneous use of simulation software: The model, approach and initial experiences. In: Cano, J., Saenz, M. (Ed.): Experimental learning in Industrial Management: Transference & Creation of Knowledge. 6th International Workshop on Simulation Games in Production Management, July 2nd–4th, 2001, Madrid, Spain, pp 9–34. Asociacion Espanola de Ingenieria de Proyectos (AEIPRO).

HIEBER, R., ALARD, R. Efficient Logistics Information Support systems for Supply Chain Management. In: Barros, L., Wehner-Hewson, N., Adjallah, S. (Ed.): International Conference on Industrial Logistics 2001, July 9th–12th, 2001, Okinawa, Japan, pp. 202–209. ICIIL-Southampton.

HINES, P., RICH, N. (1997): The Seven Value Stream Mapping Tools, International Journal of Operations & Production Management, No. 1 (1997), pp. 44–64.

HOEK v., R. (1998): Measuring the unmeasurable – measuring and improving performance in the supply chain, Supply Chain Management Volume 3 (1998) 4, pp. 187–192.

HOLMBERG, S., (2000): A Systems Perspective on Supply Chain Management, International Journal of Physical Distribution & Logistics Management, Vol. 30, No. 10, pp. 847–868.

HOULIHAN, J.B. (1985): International Supply Chain Management, International Journal of Physical Distribution & Materials Management, Vol. 15, No. 1, pp. 22–38.

JOHANNSEN, S. (2001): Concept of inventory management based on new IT systems for third party logistics, Diploma thesis, BWI ETH Zürich.

JOHANNSON, L. (1994): How Can a TQEM Approach Add Value to Your Suppy Cain?, Total Quality Environmental Management, Vol. 3, No. 4 (1994), pp. 521–530.

JOHNSON, H.T. (1990): Performance Measurement for Competitive Excellence, in Kaplan, R.S. (Ed.), Measures for Manufacturing Excellence, Harvard Business School Press, Boston, pp. 63–69.

JONES, T. C., RILEY, D. W. (1985): Using inventory for competitive advantage through supply chain management, International Journal of Physical Distribution & Materials Management, Vol. 15, No. 5 (1985), pp. 16–26.

KAHL, S. (1999): What's the "Value" of Supply Chain Software?, in: Supply Chain Management Review, Winter 1999, pp. 59–67.

KAPLAN, R., NORTON, D. (1992): The Balanced Scorecard – Measures that Drive Performance, in: Harvard Business Review, January/February 1992, pp. 71–79.

KAPLAN, R., NORTON, D. (1996): The Balanced Scorecard – Translating Strategy into Action, Harvard Business School Press, Boston.

KEITH OLIVER, R., WEBBER, M. (1982): Supply Chain Management: logistics catches up with strategy, Outlook by Booz, Allen and Hamilton Inc., 1982, in Christopher, M. (1992): Logistics: the strategic issues, Chapman & Hall, pp. 63–75.

KNOLMAYER, G., MERTENS, P., ZEIER, A. (2000): Supply Chain Management auf Basis von SAP-Systemen, Springer.

KOLATORSKI, P. (2001): Informationsplattform für die Absatzplanung, Independent Study, BWI ETH Zürich.

KUHN, A. (1998): Logistiknetze im Fokus. In: Sonderheft Fördertechnik '98. Fördermittel Journal 30 (1998), pp. 12–15.

LALONDE, B., POHLEN, T. (1996): Issues in Supply Chain Costing, in: International Journal of Logistics Management, Vol. 7, No. 1, 1996, pp. 1–12.

LAU, H.C.W., LEE, W.B. (2000): On a responsive supply chain information system, International Journal of Physical Distribution & Logistics Management, Vol. 30, No. 7/8, pp. 598–610.

LEE, H., BILLINGTON, C. (1992): Managing Supply Chain Inventory. Pitfalls and Opportunities, Sloan Management Review No. 3, Vol. 33, pp. 65–73.

LEE, H.L., PADMANABHAN, V., WHANG, S. (1997): The Bullwhip Effect in Supply Chain, Sloan Management Review (1997)1, pp. 93–102.

LUCZAK, H., EVERSHEIM, W., SCHOTTEN, M. (1998): Produktionsplanung und -steuerung, Springer.

LUMMUS, R., ALBER, K. (1997): Supply Chain Management: Balancing the Supply Chain with Customer Demand, APICS Educational & Research Foundation, Inc., (1997) 1.

LYSONS, K. (2000): Purchasing and Supply Chain Management, Prentice Hall.

MÄNNEL, B. (1996): Netzwerke in der Zulieferindustrie, Konzepte Gestaltungsmerkmale, Betriebswirtschaftliche Wirkung, DUV, Wiesbaden.

MASKELL, B.H. (1994): Performance Measurement for World Class Manufacturing, Productivity Press, Portland.

MASON-JONES, R., TOWILL, D. R. (2000): Coping with Uncertainty: Reducing Bullwhip in Supply Chains, Supply Chain Forum: An International Journal, 1, pp. 40–45.

MASON-JONES, R., TOWILL, D.R. (1997): Information Enrichment: Designing the supply chain for competitive advantage, Supply Chain Management 2 (1997) 4, pp. 137–148.

MELNYK, S., CALANTONE, R. (1999): Metrics and their Role in Supply Chain, Supply Chain Council Newsletter, 11/1999.

MERLI, G. (1991): Co-makership – the new supply strategy for manufacturers, Productivity Press, Cambridge.

MERTENS, P. (1999): Operiert die Wirtschaftsinformatik mit falschen Unternehmenszielen? – 15 Thesen, in: Becker, J., König, W., Schütte, R. et al. (Hrsg.), Wirtschaftsinformatik und Wissenschaftstheorie, Wiesbaden 1999, pp. 379–392.

MOELLER, C. (1995): Logistics Concept Development – Towards a Theory for Designing Effective Systems, Ph.D. Thesis, Aalborg University.

MÜLLER-STEWENS, G., HILLIG, A. (1992): Motive zur Bildung Strategischer Allianzen: Die aktivsten Branchen im Vergleich, in: Bronder, C./Pritzl, R. (Hrsg.): Wegweiser für Strategische Allianzen, Frankfurt und Wiesbaden 1992, pp. 64–101.

NEW, S., BURNES, B. (1997): Developing effective customer-supplier relationships: more than one way to skin a cat, International Journal of Quality & Reliability Management, 15 (4), pp. 377–388.

PFOHL, H.-C., BUSE, H.-P. (2000): Inter-organizational logistics systems in flexible production networks, International Journal of Physical Distribution & Logistics Management, Vol. 30, No. 5, pp. 338–408.

PICOT, A., FRANCK, E. (1993): Vertikale Integration. In: Hauschildt, J., Grün, O. (1993): Ergebnisse empirischer betriebswirtschaftlicher Forschung: Zu einer Realtheorie der Unternehmung. Stuttgart, pp. 179–219.

REINHART, G., WEBER, V., RUDORFER, W. (2001): Marktresponsive Supply Chains auf Basis kompetenzzentrierter Unternehmensnetzweke, Industrie Management 17, pp. 35–40.

ROSS, D.F. (1997): Competing through supply chain management: Creating market-winning strategies through supply chain partnerships, Chapman & Hall.

ROSS, S. A. (1973): The Economic Theory of Agency: The Principal's Problem, American Economic Review, Papers and Proceedings 63 (1973) 2, pp. 134–139.

RÜDIGER, M. (1998): Theoretische Grundmodelle zur Erklärung von FuE-Kooperationen. In: Zeitschrift für Betriebswirtschaft (ZfB): Betriebswirtschaftlicher Verlag Dr. Th. Gabler GmbH, Wiesbaden, 68(1998)1, pp. 25–48.

SCHMID, C. (1998): Strukturierte Gestaltung des koordinierenden Informationsflusses bei verteilter Leistungserstellung in Zuliefernetzwerken : Vorgehensweise zur konzeptionellen Auslegung zwischenbetrieblicher Informationsflüsse in der Zulieferindustrie, Diss. Techn. Wiss. ETH Zürich, Nr. 12857.

SCHOMBURG, E. (1980): Entwicklung eines betriebstypologischen Instrumentariums zur systematischen Ermittlung der Anforderungen an EDV-gestützte Produktions- und Steuerungssysteme im Maschinenbau, Diss. RWTH Aachen.

SCHÖNSLEBEN, P. (2000): Integral Logistics Management, Planning & Control of Comprehensive Business Processes, St. Lucie Press, Boca Raton.

SCHÖNSLEBEN, P., BÄRTSCHI, M., HIEBER, R. (2000): Supply Chain Management: Erfolgreicher durch Netzwerke, Manager Bilanz Nr. 1/2000, pp. 6–11.

SCHÖNSLEBEN, P., HIEBER, R. (2000): Supply Chain Management Software: Welche Erwartungshaltung ist gegenüber der neuen Generation von Planungssoftware angebracht?, io Management, Nr. 1/2 2000, pp. 18–24.

SCOR: SUPPLY-CHAIN OPERATIONS REFERENCE-MODEL, Version 4.0, August 2000, Supply Chain Council, Pittsburgh, PA, USA.

SCM-CTC: Marktstudie Supply Chain Management Software – Planungssysteme im Überblick, scm-CTC, Dortmund, Stuttgart, Zürich, 2002.

SCOTT, C., WESTBROOK, R. (1991): New Strategic Tools for Supply Chain Management, International Journal of Physical Distribution & Logistics Management, Vol. 21, No. 1, 1991, pp. 22–33.

SIMCHI-LEVI, D., KAMINSKY, P., SIMCHI-LEVI, E. (2000): Designing and Managing the Supply Chain : Concepts, Strategies, and Cases, Irwin McGraw-Hill.

SKJOETT-LARSEN, T. (2000): Third party logistics – from an interorganizational point of view, International Journal of Physical Distribution & Logistics Management, Vol. 30, No 2, pp. 112–127.

SPEKMAN, R. ET AL. (1998): An empirical investigation into supply chain management: a perspective on partnership, Supply Chain Management, Vol. 3, (1998)2, pp. 53–67.

STERMAN, J.D. (1989): Modeling managerial behavior: misconceptions of feedback in a dynamic decision-making experiment, Management Science, Vol. 355, No. 3, 1989, pp. 321–39.

STEVENS, G. (1989): Integrating the Supply Chain, Physical Distribution & Materials Management, Vol. 19, No. 8, pp. 3–8.

STUART, F. I. (1997): Supplier alliance success and failure: a longitudinal dyadic perspective. International Journal of Operations & Production, 17 (6), pp. 539–557.

SYDOW, J. (1999): Management von Netzwerkorganisationen – Zum Stand der Forschung, Betriebswirtschaftlicher Verlag Dr. Th. Gabler GmbH, Wiesbaden, pp. 279–314.

SYDOW, J. (1992): Strategische Netzwerke: Evolution und Organisation. Reihe Neue betriebswissenschaftliche Forschung, Bd. 100, Wiesbaden.

TOWILL, D. (1997) The Seamless Supply Chain – the predator's strategic advantage, International Journal of Technology Management, Vol. 14, pp. 37–55.

TURNER, R. J., (1993): Integrated Supply Chain Management: What's Wrong with this Picture?, Industrial Engineering, Vol. 25, No. 12, pp. 52–55.

VDI (1999): "Practice-oriented characteristic values for logistics in small and medium-sized companies – VDI 2525", VDI-Gesellschaft Fördertechnik Materialfluss Logistik, Düsseldorf.

VICS – Voluntary Interindustry commerce standards Association (2001): CPFR – XML Messaging Model, Draft standard for Public Comment, www.cpfr.org.

Villard, P. (2000): Supply Chain Management Concept for Key Accounts, Diploma thesis, BWI ETH Zürich.

Weber, J., Schäffer, U. (2000): Entwicklung von Kennzahlensystemen, Betriebswirtschaftliche Forschung und Praxis (BFuP), 1/2000, p. 1–16.

Westkämper, E. (1999): Die Wandlungsfähigkeit von Unternehmen, wt Werkstatttechnik 89 (1999) 4, pp. 131–140.

Wiendahl, H.P., et al. (1998): Kennzahlengestützte Prozesse im Supply Chain Management, Industrie Management 14 (1998) 6, pp. 18–24.

Wildemann (1996): H., Entwicklungsstrategien für Zulieferunternehmen, Transfer-Centrum-Verlag GmbH, München.

Williamson, O. (1985): The economic institutions of capitalism – firms, markets, relational contracting, The Free Press, New York.

Williamson, O.E. (1991): The logic of economic organization, Williamson, O.E., Winter, S.G. (Eds.), 1991, The Nature of the Firm, Oxford University Press, New York, Oxford.

Womack, J., Jones, T., Roos, D. (1990): The machine that changed the world, Rawson Associated.

Wrede, v., P. (2000): In 7 Schritten zur erfolgreichen Supply Chain, Fir+IAW-Unternehmen der Zukunft 4/2000, pp. 7–8.

Zillig, U. (1998): Integratives Logistikmanagement in Unternehmensnetzwerken: Beitrag zur Gestaltung interorganisatorischer Logistiksysteme in Produktions- und Logistiknetzwerken der Zulieferindustrie, Diss. Techn. Wiss. ETH Zürich, Nr. 12861.

Zwicky, F (1989): Morphologische Forschung – Wesen und Wandel materieller und geistiger struktureller Zusammenhänge, 82nd ed., Bäschlin, Glarus, Switzerland.

Subject index

Bold page numbers indicate the page on which a definition or explanation of the term can be found.

About the author

Dr. sc. techn. ETH Ralf Hieber, born in 1971, studied Mechanical Engineering at the University of Stuttgart (Germany) and Industrial Engineering as a scholar at the University Wisconsin/Madison (USA). He received his Master of Science (M.Sc.) in Manufacturing Systems Engineering in 1996 and his Dipl.-Ing. in Mechanical Engineering in 1997.

From 1997 to 2001, he was scientific assistant in the group of Logistics and Information Management of Prof. Dr. Paul Schönsleben at the Center for Enterprise Sciences (BWI) in the Department for Manufacturing, Industrial Engineering and Management of the Swiss Federal Institute of Technology (ETH) Zürich. He received his Ph.D. in 2001.

His research interests are in the area of value network management and information system support for transcorporate logistics processes. He served as project leader of the project ProNet from 1999 to 2001. The ideas of performance measurement in logistics networks as presented in this book were developed within this project.

Since 2001, he is senior assistant of the domain supply chain management und head of supply chain management at the Competence and Transfer Center (scm-CTC) Zurich.

Publikationen der Reihe BWI

vdf Hochschulverlag AG an der ETH Zürich